Farther Up the Strait

Coastal British Columbia Stories

Wayne J. Lutz

Powell River Books

Copyright © 2018 Wayne J. Lutz
Ingram Sparks Edition

All rights reserved. No part of this publication may be reproduced, All rights reserved. No part of this publication may be reproduced, stored in a retrieval system, or transmitted, in any form or by any means, electronic, mechanical, photocopying, recording, or otherwise, without the written prior permission of the author. Reviewers are authorized to quote short passages within a book review, as permitted under the United States Copyright Act of 1976.

Note for Librarians: a catalog record for this book that includes Dewey Decimal Classification and U.S. Library of Congress numbers is available from the Library and Archives of Canada. The complete catalog record can be obtained from their online database at:
www.collectionscanada.ca/amicus/index-e.html

ISBN 978-1-927438-28-2

Powell River Books
Powell River BC

Book sales online at:
www.powellriverbooks.com
phone: 604-483-1704
email: wlutz@mtsac.edu

10 9 8 7 6 5 4 3 2 1

To Ken...

His boating adventures inspire me –
and get me in endless trouble

The stories are true, and the characters are real.
Some details are adjusted to protect the guilty.
All of the mistakes rest solidly with the author.

Front Cover Photo:
 Theodosia Inlet at Dawn
Back Cover Photos:
 Top – Exiting Prideaux Haven, Desolation Sound
 Bottom – Westview's North Harbour, Powell River BC

Contents

Preface – After *Up the Strait*	9
1 – Theodosia	11
2 – Circumnavigating Quadra	24
3 – Okeover	46
4 – Mr. Buttercup	58
5 – Finding Gibsonites	81
Center-of-Book Photos	111
6 – Solo Voyage	115
7 – Flameout	130
8 – Squirrel Cove	145
9 – Engine Change	157
10 – Gorge Harbour	179
11 – Von Donop	196
Epilogue – Getting Out There	215
Geographic Index	217

Wayne J. Lutz

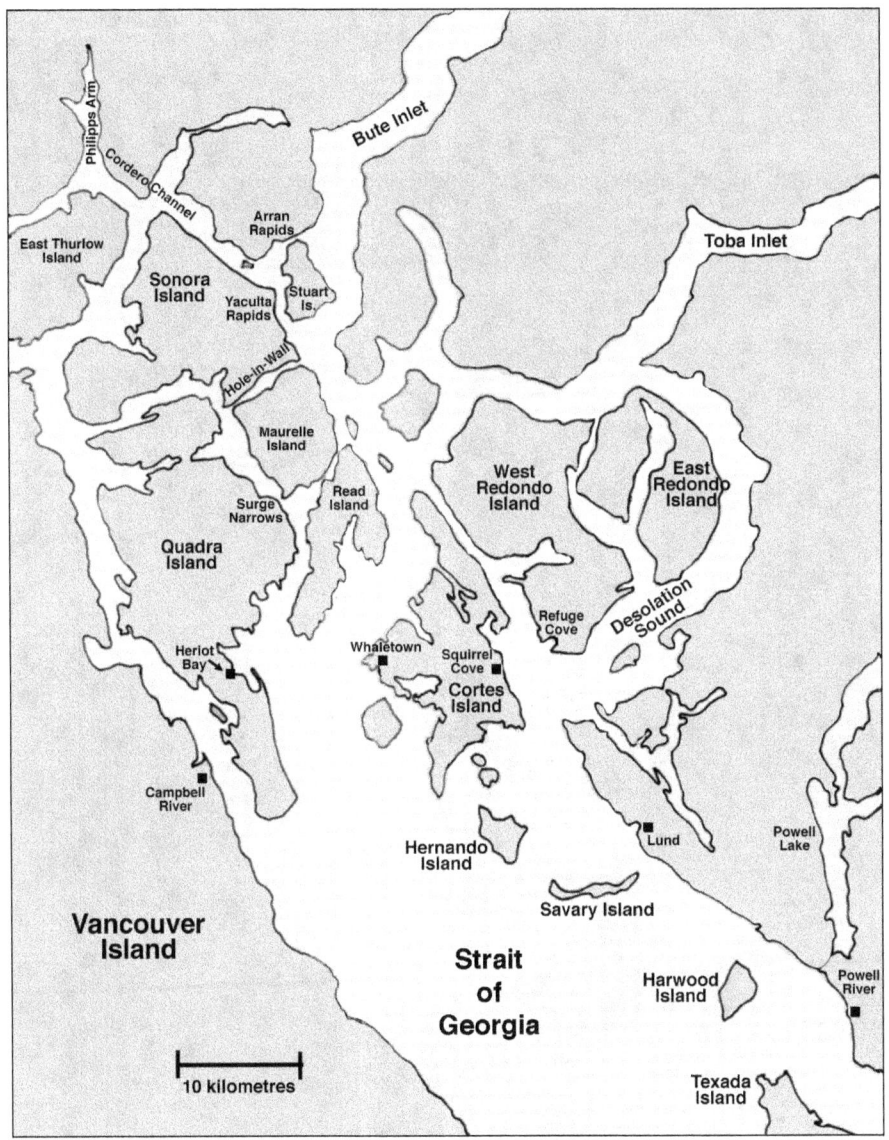

Regional Overview

Farther Up the Strait

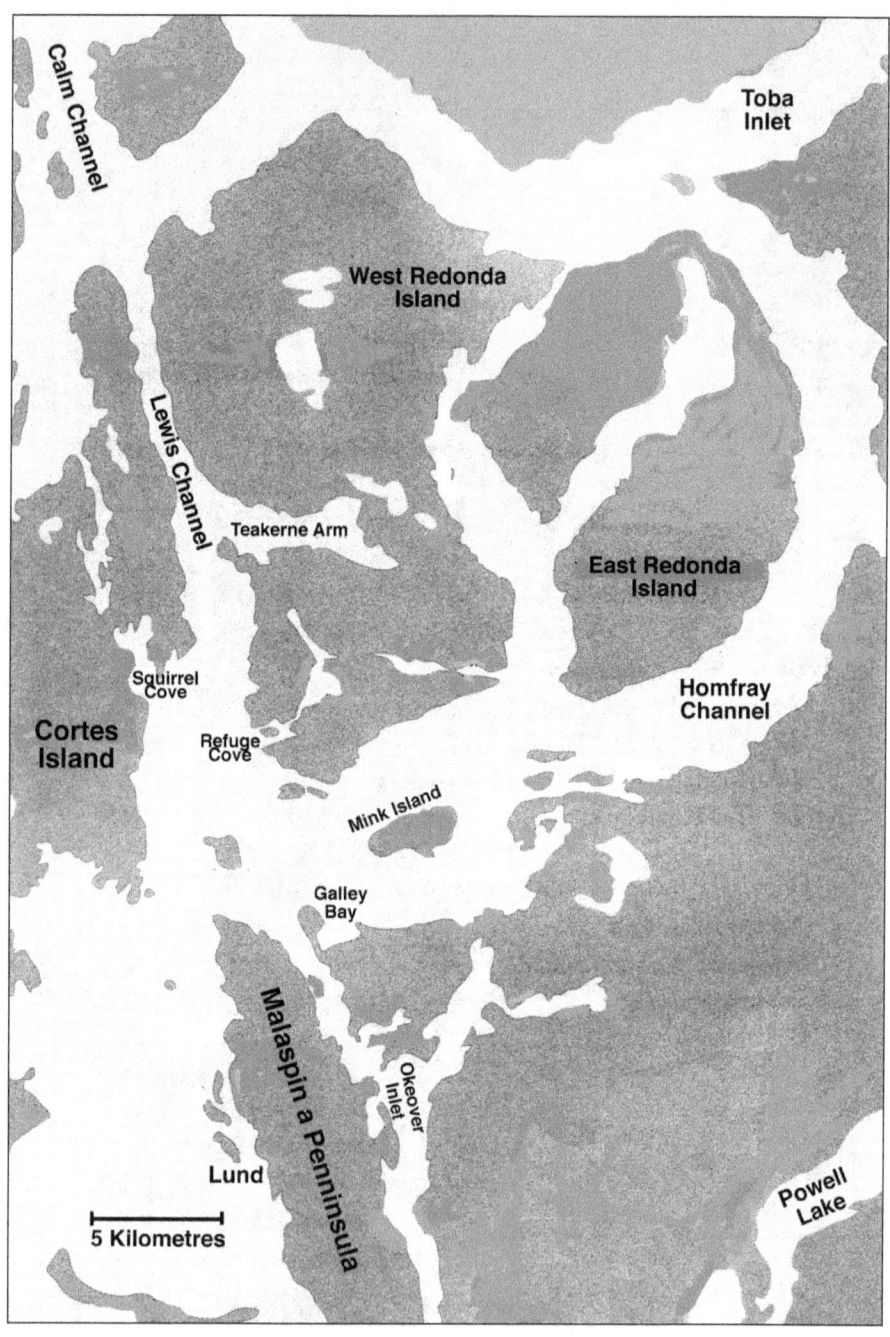

Desolation Sound

Wayne J. Lutz

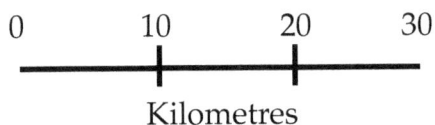

Lower Coastal British Columbia

Farther Up the Strait

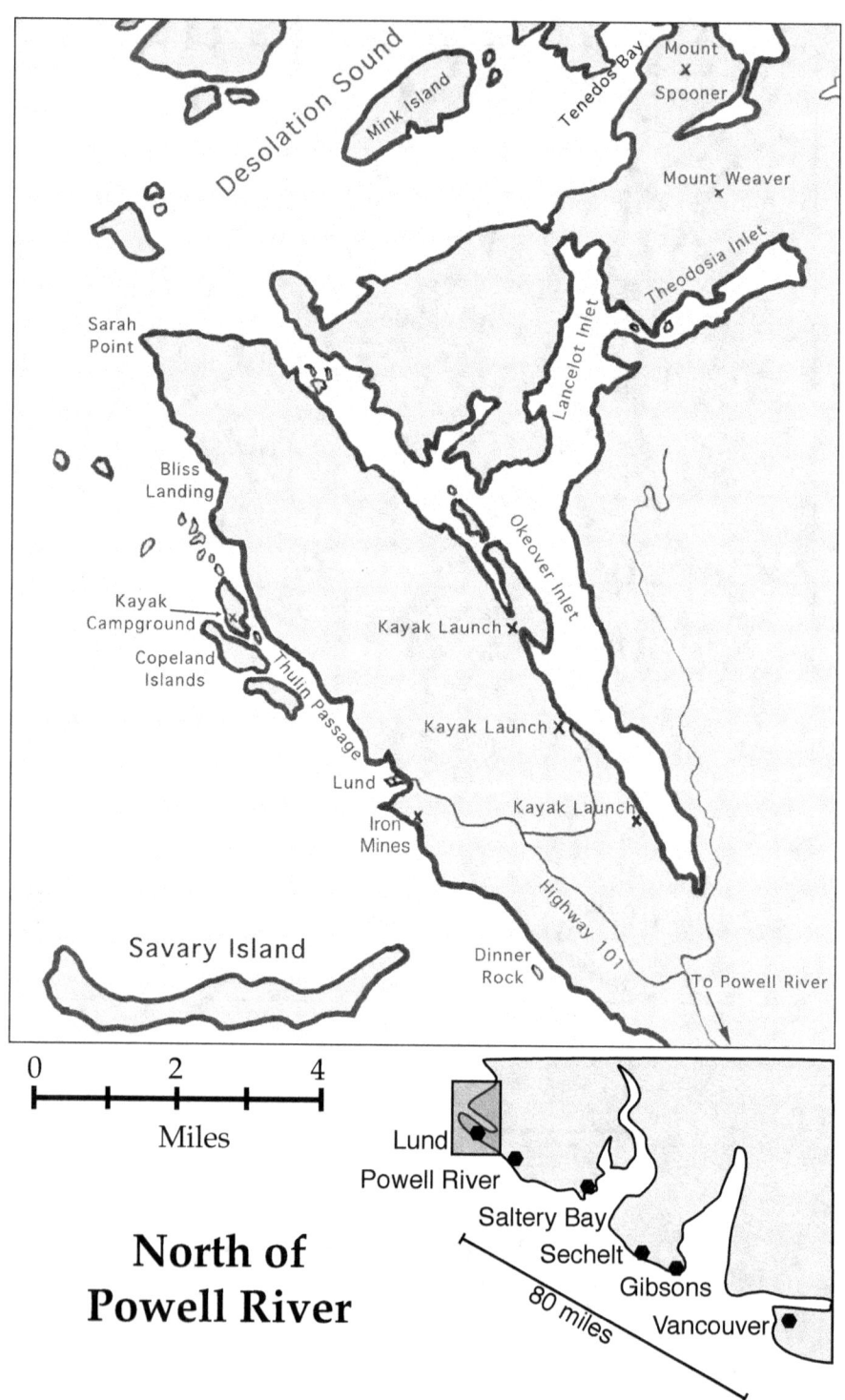

North of Powell River

Preface

After *Up the Strait*

As a relatively new boater, my first book about the Strait of Georgia, *Up the Strait*, led to ideas for a follow-up volume. It was only logical to write about adventures farther north into the Broughton Archipelago and the big inlets documented in renowned cruising travelogues like *The Curve of Time*. The prospective book was to be called *Up the Inlet*, a taste of places north of Desolation Sound. But, at least for now, it was not to be.

The delay wasn't because of lack of places to explore or a declining desire to go farther north. Instead, it was because of the glorious places in the Strait of Georgia that I had not yet explored. These coves and tucked-away anchorages are sometimes categorized as "gunkholes," a name both fitting (quiet anchorages) and misleading (dangerous to navigate). Many of these magnificent destinations are true inlets (Okeover, Lancelot, and Theodosia), though they somehow don't rank in size with the better-known arms farther north (Toba, Bute, Knight, and other giant fjords). So for now, I decided to concentrate on the remainder of the Strait of Georgia, while reaching north to the islands of Quadra, Cortes, Read, Stuart, and Sonora. The book needed a new name, so *Farther Up the Strait* was born.

My 24-foot Bayliner, *Halcyon Days*, has proven itself to be an ideal boat for exploration of the mini-inlets and islands of the northern reaches of the Strait of Georgia. Originally purchased as a transitional vessel that would need to be upsized for the real challenges of the BC coast, I soon began to refer to *Halcyon Days* as the "perfect boat." Sure, it's small by ocean-going standards, but its compact design fits me fine. How could I ever leave this boat behind for something bigger? Good question, and I haven't found an answer yet. So it will remain the star of my boating books, including the next volume that will be entitled (and this time I'm serious) *Up the Inlet.*

Chapter 1

Theodosia

To boaters on the west coast of British Columbia, the word "inlet" conjures up images of huge swathes of water snaking inland between high mountains. The majestic serenity of Jervis Inlet to the south of Powell River and Toba to the north clearly fit into this category. Even closer is the sometimes-disregarded chain of inlets that begins with Okeover, then Lancelot, and finally Theodosia, each leading into the next. Powell River residents don't place them in the same category as Bute and Kingcome, partly because they are local and easily access. They are shorter, too. Yet, lined end-to-end (as you navigate them), they form a local getaway that's as awe inspiring as the more famous inlets farther north.

In one of my first solo trips in the Bayliner (*Up the Main*, Chapter 8), I followed the Okeover-Lancelot-Theodosia path. Memories of that trip focus on an octopus, the towering walls of Lancelot, a feisty dogfish, and the initial letdown of Theodosia as I imagined it.

How could a place as universally beautiful as Theodosia be a letdown? Answer: our minds create expectations. When these visions are not realized, it leads to disenchantment. I had heard so much about Theodosia Inlet (and nothing about Lancelot) that I was primed for disappointment. Entering Lancelot Inlet, I was immediately shocked by the unexpected beauty of the fjord-like inlet. Theodosia, of which my friend, John, speaks with such majestic respect, was an easy target for disappointment. After winding through the challenging entry, Theodosia greeted me like a plain-Jane large lake. Where were the vast vertical walls and huge trees?

Two years later, another trip up these inlets seemed appropriate. Theodosia was now an esteemed destination. My repeated visits were not by boat. Instead, I rode my quad into Theo, and each visit revealed more of the broad valley's beauty. Theodosia is an inlet, and it's a valley. It's also magical.

* * * * *

Margy is at the helm on the command bridge, maneuvering out of Westview Harbour in the Bayliner, while I kneel on the forward deck, lashings our docking lines to the rails. It's early June, still too early for the main northward flux of summer cruisers. Today's forecast calls for 22 degrees C, with light northwest winds. Perfect for an overnighter on the chuck.

As we clear the breakwater, I use the narrow catwalk to climb around the cabin, hanging onto the handrails along the command bridge. Then I climb up from the aft deck, three steps to the bridge.

Everything about this boat is small in comparison to the normal inlet cruisers. It's a 23.5-foot Bayliner Monterey, vintage 1987, and nicely modified by the previous owner for added comforts, including lots of storage space and a superb electrical system. The beam width is 8 feet, and the dingy is a fiberglass catamaran design (*Mr. Bathtub*), mounted on hefty rear swim-grid latches.

The Bayliner rides comfortably in seas up to 3 feet, but it can handle bigger waves, if you're willing. The stern-drive is powered by a twenty-year-old gas engine that still runs smoothly, starts fine (except when extremely cold), and burns almost no oil. The Bayliner may not be as big as most boats that challenge the coast of BC, but it's a wonderful boat.

John purchased this boat for me (no harbour space available for a boat of greater length), and now he wants us to move up to something larger. We're on the waiting list for a bigger mooring spot. But how could I do that to *Halcyon Days*? She has served me well. It would be nearly impossible to sell this boat under any circumstances. She's the perfect boat. Just not perfect for all sea conditions, nor does it have the diesel engine I covet.

"Make it go," I say, as I plop down on the upholstered bench seat next to Margy.

She smoothly pushes the throttle forward, and the Bayliner slowly accelerates.

And it is slowly. I've noticed the boat does not come up on-plane quickly today, with a winter's growth of algae and assorted marine critters on the lower hull. But we've been on several trips on the chuck in recent weeks, and the stern leg and upper hull are considerably cleaner because of this activity. Still, the bottom of the boat remains thick with drag-producing marine life. The boat slogs her way up to speed, especially with our full fuel load.

Margy adjusts the trim switches towards their bow-up position, but we're pushing water too slowly to come up to our normal cruising speed of 22 knots.

"Not on-plane yet," I criticize. It's not her fault – the critters are just too thick. "Try maximum power until we're fully up."

Normally, full power isn't needed to accelerate to cruise configuration. A notch lower on the throttles is certainly better for the engine.

"The bottom looks cleaner lately," says Margy. "At least the part we can see."

"But the keel isn't as smooth as it was," I complain. "The bottom paint is designed to come loose when the critters build up, but then things begin to go from bad to worse."

Once the hull paint breaks down, the critters accumulate uncontested, and drag increases exponentially.

I hear the dual-carbs kick in as Margy accelerates past the soft spot where the engine hesitates momentarily from the overly-rich fuel. Then it feels like we're more distinctly on-plane, but just barely.

"Now try bow-up," I say, typically bossy. "Then come back a touch on the power."

Margy adjusts the trim switches and comes back on the throttle until we hear a softer RPM. We trudge along barely on the step. I'd like to check our speed, but the GPS is back at the factory for warranty repairs. It feels like a bit less than 20 knots, which explains the mushy feel.

"It's a lot like an airplane," I explain in my flight instructor mode. "The hull looks smooth, but it's similar to a dirty wing or one with too many rivets. Once the bottom paint starts to fall off, there goes the laminar flow."

One thing for sure, boats have a lot in common with airplanes. It's amazing how comfortable the transition has been for me. All of the same factors are pertinent: weather, propulsion systems (props too!), electrical and mechanical subsystems, and even aerodynamics. When you catch the ideal drift during a smooth approach to a dock, the water feels like air cushioning an airplane's wing during a perfect landing. In a plane, you ease back gradually on the wheel to feel the increased angle of attack and the thickening air of aerodynamic ground effect. Squeak, squeak – you're down. Bump, bump, you're against the dock. Still, my landing flares are a lot better than my dock arrivals. Then again, my logbook shows 7000 hours of flying.

For an airplane with a dirty wing, the solution to a problem like this is simple and quick. A wash and wax will do wonders to improve airfoil performance. For a boat, you need to remove it from the water, clean and sand the hull, and repaint it. Cleaning a boat's hull rather than an airplane's wing is much more manpower intense, but the change in performance is also considerably more noticeable.

We continue up the strait past Harwood Island's sand spit, giving it a wide berth. We're more conservative without our GPS for accurate depth contours. Then we cruise past Dinner Rock and Lund. As we approach the Copeland Islands, we see two sailboats and a powerboat traveling together into Thulin Passage.

"Gibsonites," says Margy.

"Oh, you're right. Do you recognize any of them?"

The group from Gibson Yacht Club left Powell River this morning. We saw them from our condo balcony as they departed Westview Harbour as a group, headed north on their annual voyage. From the condo, I took a photo of some of their boats as they departed, and immediately emailed it to my friend, Ken, in Gibsons. When he's unable to travel with the group (as on this trip), he likes to keep track of their progress.

"It looks like Klaus' boat, the Uniflite," notes Margy. "I don't recognize the other two, but I bet it's the Gibsonites."

"Creep up on them a bit more, and I'll get a picture for Ken."

That's easy to do. They travel at less than 8 knots, whether under sail or power. Today their sails are down, and the husky Uniflite powerboat, crewed by Klaus and Fran, chugs along with them on it's two small, fuel-efficient diesels.

I snap the photo, and then we veer off to the outside of the Copeland Islands. In Thulin Passage, particularly with all of these boats now entering, we'd need to slow to no-wake speed, but outside the islands we can go full bore. Today, full bore is a bit sluggish.

We swing around the Copelands and then angle towards Sarah Point. The entrance to Okeover is right around the corner.

"I'll be downstairs for awhile," I tell Margy. She nods, and I climb down the steps to the aft deck and then into the cabin.

At the chart table inside, I check the tide tables. It's not critical, but I'd like to know what to expect as we enter Okeover Inlet. The maximum current here is never dangerous, if handled with respect. But it's noticeable and fun to play with. On this entry, we can expect maximum tidal flow, flooding into Okeover, so that should produce noticeable swirling in the narrower areas, coupled with a perceptible push.

I climb up to the command bridge again, and plop down next to Margy. We pass through the narrowest portion of Okeover's entrance at

reduced power. Just beyond the entry island, small whirlpools appear to each side of the Bayliner,. Then the passage opens up again, and Margy increases power. I look back toward the entrance and watch the wake of the Bayliner peel off to both sides, one of my favourite sights from the bridge.

We round the point into Lancelot Inlet, and I await the fjord-like terrain. It never arrives.

Lancelot is somehow different on this trip. Maybe it's the position of our boat in the center of the channel. But more likely it's my mood, rather than the angle of the view. On my earlier visit to Lancelot, I was expecting nothing, and received towering cliffs and a feeling of isolation that became magnified in my mind. Today I expect majesty and am greeted by mere tranquil beauty. It feels like the geology has changed, which is highly unlikely in less than two years.

In what seems like only a few minutes, we're at the entrance to Theodosia. This is where, on a previous solo voyage, I wound through carefully with the Bayliner at mid-tide, to be greeted by a show-off crew boat from the logging camp. I remember it veering around me, on-plane while I crawled through the river-like channel at near-idle.

Today this winding body of connecting water flows more beautiful than I remember. Maybe this is because I'm more relaxed about the entry. Experience brings confidence, allowing my eyes to wander to the sublimity of the terrain.

Just as we pass the narrowest section of the entrance, the Bayliner traveling at minimum throttle, it's deja vu. Here comes a blue-and-silver crew boat, headed directly at us. The workboat is at full throttle, and we're at creeping-throttle. Margy starts to turn to the side.

"Just hold here, and let him maneuver around us," I suggest.

Margy shifts into neutral (easy when you're already at idle), and we wait.

The blue-and-silver boat continues directly for us.

"Going to give us a thrill!" I exclaim.

"Are you sure he sees us?" asks Margy hesitantly.

I notice her hand rests on the shift lever, ready for action, if needed.

"Oh, he sees us alright. Probably muttering something about 'damn tourists,' I bet."

"Maybe 'damn Americans' instead."

She's right – I'm thinking the same thing, but we fly a BC flag. Still, sometimes I think Canadian workboats can tell we're American novices by some form of telepathy.

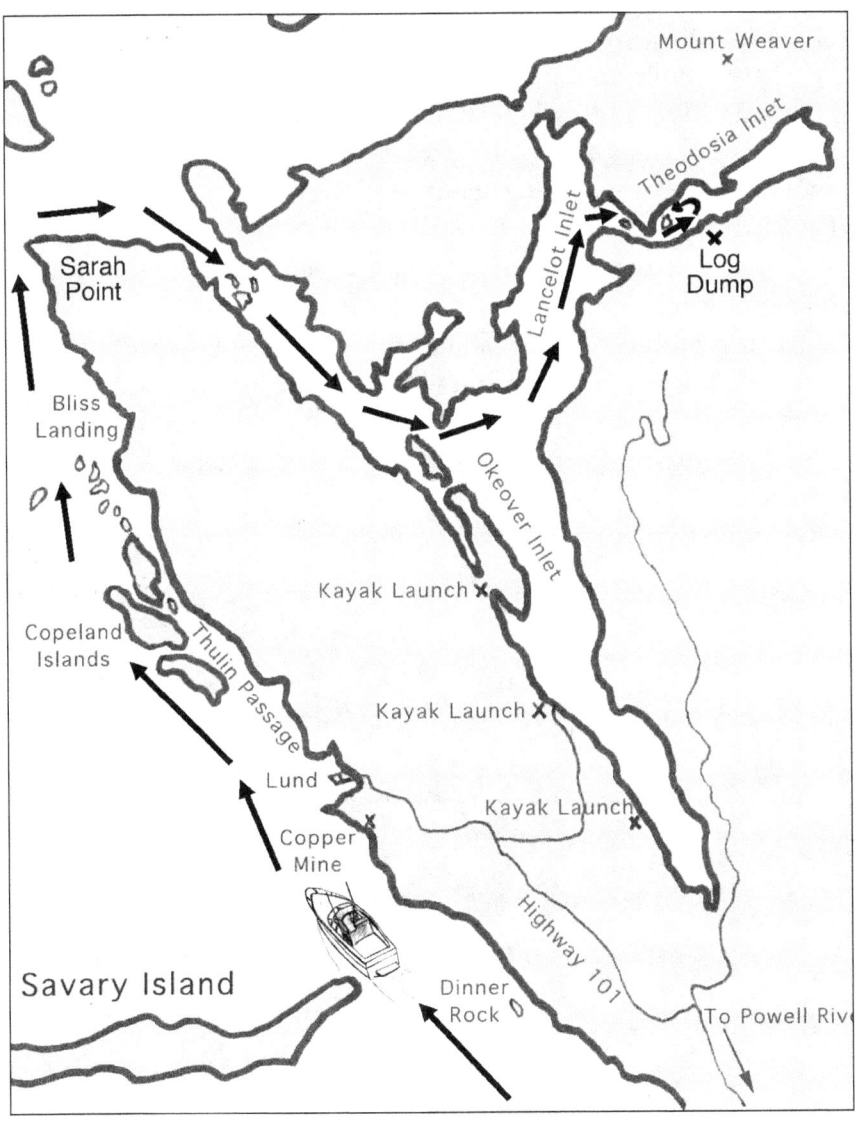

Vroom! In a flash of spray, the crew boat's captain puts the shiny hull into a steep banking turn to the left and whooshes around us. I wave jubilantly at the show we're provided. The boat turns sharply back into the center of the narrow passage. He knows these waters, and he knows how to toy with us. As the boat winds through the narrowest part of the passage at full-cruise power, it's a sight of beauty.

"Maybe he didn't see us until the last minute," says Margy.

"Yeah, right."

I have a smile on my face as big as a kid on a carnival ride.

Margy shifts back into forward, and we creep out into the wider opening of Theodosia Inlet. It's a marvelous and surprising panorama.

"I remember you writing about this," says Margy. "You referred to it as a big boring lake."

"I did. But that must have been a different place, or at least a different time."

There's nothing boring about this spot. Mountains surround Theodosia Inlet to the north and west. And the logging slash we drop down through on our quads angles up sharply to the east. It's amazing to see this often-ridden trail area from the perspective of the inlet's entrance.

The logging dock is busy. Besides the crew boat that has just departed, two other workboats are moored here. A truck with a bed full of logs is approaching the steeply-sloped ramp. We stop about 100 metres offshore and await the action. We only need to wait a few minutes.

A yellow skip-loader pushes at the load from the other side of the logging truck, which is now parked parallel to the shore. The yellow vehicle revs its engine, and logs begin to tilt towards the angled ramp as a single pile. Then something goes wrong.

A log at the top falls off the truck at an awkward angle. It falls with one end to the ground and the other still at the top of the pile. We're a bit too far away to tell exactly what's happening. Before I can pull the binoculars out of their case, the skip-loader revs its engine again.

The errant log is still tilted onto the ground, but the rest of the mass drags it along for the ride. The whole mass of logs slides down the 45-degree ramp, tumbling into the water with a huge splash. Moments later, we hear the time-delayed crashing sound of wood meeting water with tremendous force.

After watching this unique event, we drop anchor in shallow water near the mouth of the inlet. It's a small bay that allows our anchor to settle in 30 feet of water. The hook grabs promptly, and we swing comfortably, tucked in behind a peninsula that's nearly cutoff from shore. At high tide, we can see across the narrow isthmus, watching crew boats as they enter and leave Theodosia through the channel on the other side.

From this fine observation spot, we watch the activities near the logging dock. Cranes, logging trucks, and a variety of support vehicles move around the area, with the occasional big show – another dump of logs. After the first drop, things get even more exciting. Subsequent trucks use another dump site, without a ramp. The yellow skip-loader pushes bundles of logs directly off the truck and into the water. It's a 10-metre drop, and a hell of a splash.

The load malfunction we initially witnessed turns out to be common. Often, one or more logs temporarily hang at first-push, and each time there's a brief pause and reevaluation of the situation. Then the yellow vehicle revs its engine and gives a second push. The logs roll off the truck, flounder awkwardly for a few moments, and fall to the water with a giant splash, The delayed sound that reaches us a few seconds later is a bonus to the event.

What if the logs don't break free of the truck as they tumble? How often is a logging truck flung into the chuck?

It's a constant performance, until 4 pm, when the blue-and-silver crew boat begins several trips out of the inlet and then back in to pickup more loggers. Another silver-only workboat also makes several runs.

With the logging operation temporarily closed down, it's very quiet. There are no other boats in Theodosia this evening, and the feeling of isolation is enchanting. The June sun rides high, and this is a good time to write, but the sunlight overwhelms my laptop screen. So I crawl into the forward V-berth, open the overhead hatch, and hang a T-shirt from the opening to shade my computer.

Meanwhile, Margy casts her fishing lure into the shallow water.

"Do you think there are salmon here?" she yells from the aft deck.

"Probably. But it's awfully shallow in this bay. Maybe you'll catch a nice dogfish."

There's no such thing as a nice dogfish. I remember my unpleasant battle with a dogfish in this inlet two years ago (*Up the Main*, Chapter 8). Sure enough, and deja vu again – she catches a big fighting fish on one of her first casts. I pop out of the V-berth to watch the action.

This is a big fish. It could be a salmon, after all. The fish runs under the boat.

"Keep him away from the prop," I instruct.

Easier said than done. This fish is going wherever it wants.

As Margy tries to reel in her catch, I reach over and adjust the drag setting on the front of her reel. When the fish runs with the lure, it bends the pole substantially, even with the drag set liberally.

Finally, she brings the fish near the surface, and I think it's a salmon. Then it darts under the boat again. The next time it comes near the surface, we can see that it's a large dogfish. Its shark's jaw is ominous, with scary teeth that I'll need to combat with my pliers to remove the hook The fish has a shiny purplish-maroon top and a near-white belly. But most of my attention is focused on its vicious-looking mouth.

Finally, I'm able to assist by grabbing the fishing line near the end of the pole. I raise the dogfish high enough to clasp the hook with my pliers. The barbless hook is the saving grace, since I don't want to be around this mouth for long. On first grab, I twist the pliers quickly and simultaneously shake the hook and the heavy fish. The metre-long dogfish slips off under his own weight. It's a mighty splash and a sore jaw for the fish, but he'll heal quickly. The dogfish darts nearly strait down and immediately out of sight.

While on the aft deck, I assemble the Kemmerer bottle by stringing a rope through the central tube and attach a 5-pound weight on a 2-foot leading piece of rope. This is the metal water sample bottle I used for the Powell Lake deep-drop in *Up the Strait*.

I drop the bottle over the side of the boat, wait for the heavy weight to hit bottom, and then attach the metal messenger weight and drop it down the rope. I feel the messenger make firm contact with the bottle, slamming the valves shut and capturing the water at the bottom. Then I haul the bottle and weights back into the boat.

I drain water from the spring-release drain on the bottom of the bottle, using three small pill bottles. After waiting for the samples to settle for an hour, I setup my microscope in the cabin and prepare a slide, using two drops of water from one of the sample bottles.

The results are disappointing. With the sun still above the horizon, the light in the cabin is bright and rapidly changing as the boat swings on anchor. In the microscope, the field of view brightens quickly and then fades. Flashes of light in the lens make it impossible to see much detail. So I give up and wait for sunset.

Later that evening, when the brightness problem no longer exists, I use the battery-powered microscope light for illumination, scanning another slide from a second sample bottle. But there isn't a lot to see. There's definite plant life here, but I find no movement. If there's animal life, it shows no motion. I scan the slide completely, finding only a few nondescript greenish-yellow blobs. Even at high magnification, the form of these plants is less structured than my samples from near the surface of Powell Lake.

* * * * *

That night, I sleep well, as I usually do in the V-berth. This boat is as steady as a rock, even in light winds. Tonight we swing on the anchor under a gentle breeze. The sound of water slapping lightly at the hull provides a gentle lullaby.

As is usual for me, I awaken early in the morning, just as light begins to filter into the cabin. I check my watch. It's a few minutes before 4 am, and already dawn is in progress. The longest day of the year is only two weeks away, and the sun is poking its light upward from the northeast horizon at this early hour.

I step out onto the aft deck. The sky is partly cloudy. To the northeast, twilight paints a panorama of colour, with reflections of the mountains in the water. I relax in a cloth camp chair on the deck, while the Bayliner gently swings on her anchor. I pull a red hoodie over my head – huge yellow "USC" letters on the front – sliding it down, raising the hood, and tightening the drawstring around my neck.

The air is cool and damp, not cold. I sit comfortably in my temporary cocoon, watching the dawn as it slowly grows from the northeast horizon. Birds chirp, awakened by the early light. Dawn in Theodosia. Can there be a more beautiful spot in this world?

◊ ◊ ◊ ◊ ◊ ◊ ◊

Chapter 2

Circumnavigating Quadra

The morning begins fast and efficiently. My alarm awakens me a few minutes before 8 o'clock, and I flip on the FM radio to hear the long-range weather forecast. Outside the float cabin, it's brilliantly clear, and the next three days should be nearly perfect for mid-August, to be followed by a return to the showery conditions of the past few days.

I climb down the stairs from the loft, light the stove to begin boiling water to wash the dishes stacked on the counter, and begin packing up for a trip to town and then out on the chuck in the Bayliner.

Margy hears me fumbling downstairs, and knows the plan. She probably heard the long-range forecast too, along with the rattling of the pots and pans, and knows we're headed to town. In a few minutes she climbs down the stairs and takes over dishwashing duties, a small stack from last night. Preparing to leave our wonderful home anytime, for any reason, is a difficult task, and I know Margy is distressed by this even more than I am. She loves the sunshine on the floating deck. But there should be plenty everywhere in coastal BC over the next few days.

I pull the tin boat up onto the dock, chain it to the deck, and remove the drain plug. Then I turn off the cabin's electrical power, and help Margy close the drapes and blinds. Within 45 minutes of this morning's alarm, we're in the Campion and motoring out of Hole in the Wall. Very efficient, with little visible resistance from a still-drowsy Margy – a good start.

At the Shinglemill, we take everything ashore in one load, another sign of today's orderly beginning. Any trip to or from the cabin with only one load to carry is an accomplishment.

We stop for breakfast on the way into town, buying some to-go snacks for the Bayliner. Even with three days of traveling on the chuck, we'll be in good shape with a few fresh food items and lots of cold drinks. The boat's pantry has a stock of dry goods that'll last us a long time, and we can easily get by without fresh meat. Most who cruise the chuck look at their travels as an opportunity for a good grilled steak and hearty meals on the deck of their boat. We like such a lifestyle too, but it would mean an extra trip to the grocery store. Besides, nearly every day, we have barbecue picnics on the deck of our floating cabin. So we'll be food-efficient on this trip.

Margy parks her truck in the two-hour zone in front of the condo, a sure sign we plan to get going soon. If only we can survive the remaining obstacle to pre-trip efficiency – what I call the Big "I" problem, the Internet. When Margy and I get on the Internet, particularly after several days absence, it's difficult to wrap things up quickly.

"How's an hour sound?" I ask, as we enter the elevator.

"Sounds okay. I'll be ready," replies Margy.

Meaning: it's a tough challenge, but I can do it if you can.

I allocate my hour for specific tasks – get the computer running; download email while taking a quick shower; unpack what little I've brought from the cabin; repack a bag for the chuck; check the updated marine forecast; and then it's back to the computer to deal with the email. I also flip on the TV to the Weather Network, paying attention to the long-range charts, which are easy to absorb while dealing with the Big "I."

Margy allocates her time similarly, posting a mini-notice to her Internet blog and answering her email. She takes care of her accepted task of filling the soft-sided ice chest with ice packs and cold drinks, and bundling up some books for sales opportunities along the way.

My tasks include packing some specialized items: binoculars, guide books, recently purchased fishing equipment, and some new docking lines. We make our self-imposed one-hour deadline with a few minutes to spare. The biggest accomplishment is getting past the Big "I" without either of us getting bogged down.

* * * * *

At 12:20, we're ready to start the Bayliner's engine, a fact I can precisely document because that's the time I take off my watch and place it on the boat's chart table. I'm getting good at avoiding watches, but I'll need mine later when we're trying to coordinate our entrance to tidal passages along the way.

Outside the harbour, boats are everywhere. Almost all are pleasure boats, a rare situation here, except during the height of summer. Most are headed south, with the start of school only a few weeks away. Slow cruisers and sailboats need to start homeward from their northerly ports of call, if they are to get the kids home in time for school. Many are already passing Powell River on their trek down the strait.

The sea is nearly calm, and the sky is cloudless, with a temperature forecast promising highs in the low 20s. That's not particularly unusual for mid-August. There have been few hot days this summer, with only one brief period with temperatures above 30. July was one of the coolest and rainiest on record.

"Are you still sorry we left our cabin?" I ask.

"No, this is gorgeous," replies Margy. "But you know how hard it is to drag me off the float in any kind of weather. Once I get going, I'm okay."

The command bridge is perfect for cruising today – not quite cool enough to need a long-sleeve shirt, and a smooth path of water ahead. We don't have a destination for tonight, but that's fine. It's always fun to just start north, and see what happens. Summer-season anchoring can be a crowded affair in many places, but we'll try to avoid the more popular spots. The steady southward flow of boats provides encouragement that there are plenty of quiet anchorages to be found. The farther north we go, the less crowded it should become.

As we approach Lund, boats maneuver in all directions. Although many trek south, two Savary Island water taxis cross in front of us, and numerous other work boats are entering and leaving the Lund Harbour. Farther ahead, I can see several masts near the entry to Thulin Passage, so I alter course towards the outside of the Copeland Islands where we can keep up our speed without interfering with other traffic.

As we angle out from Lund, I glance into the harbour, trying to judge the level of activity at the fuel dock. It's impossible to see the details, but one large trawler and a smaller boat take up one entire side of the dock. Summer hasn't been very prosperous for seaside businesses, partly aggravated by the poor early summer weather, coupled with rising fuel prices. Most importantly, as they say, it's the economy, stupid.

Once past the Copeland Islands, I aim just to the left of Sarah Point, a heading that will take us nearly direct to our fuel stop at Refuge Cove. We don't really need fuel, but it's a good chance to top off and check on book sales at the general store.

During the summer, it's difficult to refuel without being asked to move your boat from the dock immediately afterwards. Parking is that crowded. But today, I can buy Margy some time by getting gas, while she walks up to the store to check on the status of my books. It's also a great excuse for me to avoid the business aspects of my book company. After all, someone has to pump the gas and provide the getaway vehicle.

Near Sarah Point, on this slightly rippled ocean, two jet skiers come up on our right side out of nowhere. They blast on by at nearly three times our speed.

"Must be Malcolm and Mike," I say.

"Wouldn't be surprised," Margy replies.

It's not implausible that these adventurers are Malcolm and Mike. They use their Sea-Doos like motorcycles on the highway, jetting everywhere. If a boat can go there, so too can they, except faster. Recently they traveled up Jervis Inlet all the way to the head, a journey of major proportions in any boat. To do it on a jet ski seems impossible. Coming home, in Jervis' up-inlet afternoon waves, it almost became a voyage of disaster. But they made it.

"Maybe they're headed for Bute Inlet," I joke.

You don't see a lot of jet skiers off Sarah Point, and this huge region is amazingly small when it comes to seeing people you know. So it really could be Malcom and Mike. Such encounters are one of the many small-world aspects of the BC coast.

In a few minutes, the jet skis are out of sight. As we pass the entrance to Desolation Sound, boats are crisscrossing in all directions. It isn't a heavy parade, but it does surprise me for a weekday, even in August.

Directly ahead of us, a scattered armada of boats is converging on Refuge Cove. Even from this distance, it's obvious that all is well with the pleasure boating industry, regardless of a wet summer and high fuel prices.

"Shouldn't be hard to find Refuge Cove today," says Margy.

"No, but wait until you see the gas line."

As we enter the cove, a large yacht is just exiting. A seaplane also blasts out, going airborne right opposite us. We follow a sailboat in, trailing it until it veers off to the left towards the transient dock. We're now second in line for fuel dock space. And it is a line – the gas dock is currently full, with another boat about our size waiting for parking. When a boat pulls out on the right side, he swings around to take that berth. In just a few minutes, another boat exits on the left side, and we pull around a large trawler to take the vacant spot.

"Once we're docked, you can head up to the store," I say. "If they make me leave before you're back, I'll be looking for you at the transient dock and get you aboard somehow."

"No problem," says Margy. "A publicist's work is never done."

She takes the book sales jobs without complaint. Maybe it's partly because she knows how grumpy I get when our small business takes over my life. In any case, I appreciate not having to deal with people I

don't know regarding book promotion, and she does the job well. Her "publicist" title is something we've adopted in deference to the small size of our book company.

As soon as our lines are tied, Margy heads for the store. I wait for the fuel attendant to approach me, since this provides additional time for Margy to complete her task. Now that the Bayliner is at the fuel dock, the pace of things seems much slower than I've seen during previous summers. In fact, two more boats have now departed on the far side of the fueling area, and no vessels have taken their place. When I finally walk around the corner towards the fuel attendant's office, the two jet skis that passed us are tied up to the dock, and the riders are talking to boaters parked behind them. It's not Malcom and Mike, so that proves that others use their jet skis like motorcycles in the channels and straits.

"Oh, need gas?" says the fuel attendant as he comes out of his office, nearly bumping into me.

"Sure, but no hurry."

The fuel attendant doesn't look in a hurry either. I motion to the other side of the dock where the Bayliner is parked, and he walks leisurely around to the pump on that side.

"Been busy?" I ask, as he hands me the hose.

"Fairly good these past few weeks. Real busy today."

"It's got me concerned," I say. "Today there are boats everywhere, but it doesn't seem like the summer has been so good."

I've learned that fuel attendants at docks everywhere have a better handle on the pulse of boating traffic than anyone else. They notice the differences from week to week and year to year.

"July was a weather disaster," says the gas attendant, seemingly not tempted to go back to any other boats that need attention.

"Maybe the price of gas, too, don't you think?" I say.

"Not really. I think it's mostly the weather. We're hoping they'll stay out a bit longer this year to make up for July."

"But school begins in a few weeks," I note.

"True, but maybe those without kids will stay out later in August, even early September."

Finally, the attendant wanders away to see what's happening on the other side of the dock. The big boat parked behind me has already pumped his fuel, and no one seems to be pressuring him to get going. So I pump the gas slowly, giving Margy plenty of time at the store.

When I'm finished, I take care of my bill in the office, and then walk around the dock, looking at boats and avoiding getting aboard the Bayliner. In a few minutes, I see Margy starting down the steep ramp from shore. No one asks me to leave, so I relax and take in the scenery. The jet skiers depart, and now the fuel dock is nearly empty, except for me and two big boats that seem abandoned.

"All of the copies of *Up the Strait* were gone, so they bought five more," says Margy. "You've sure got a good publicist."

"The best!"

* * * * *

We now have a plan. From here, we'll follow Lewis Channel north to the top of Cortes Island. On the way up the channel, we'll pass through an area where there are usually visible currents that are easily navigated on-plane.

Once at the top of Cortes, we'll be able to turn west through Sutil Channel to Heriot Bay, where can take on fuel that will last us for a complete circumnavigation of Quadra Island. Then we can continue north along the east side of Quadra to the other Hole in the Wall – the one that's more well known to mariners than our paradise on Powell lake. If the timing is right, we can poke our heads into this famous channel near slack tide, before continuing around Quadra. Alternatively, we can slip through Hole in the Wall into Calm Channel near Bute Inlet, and then home through Desolation Sound. So we have two good plans to choose from, and both sound like fun.

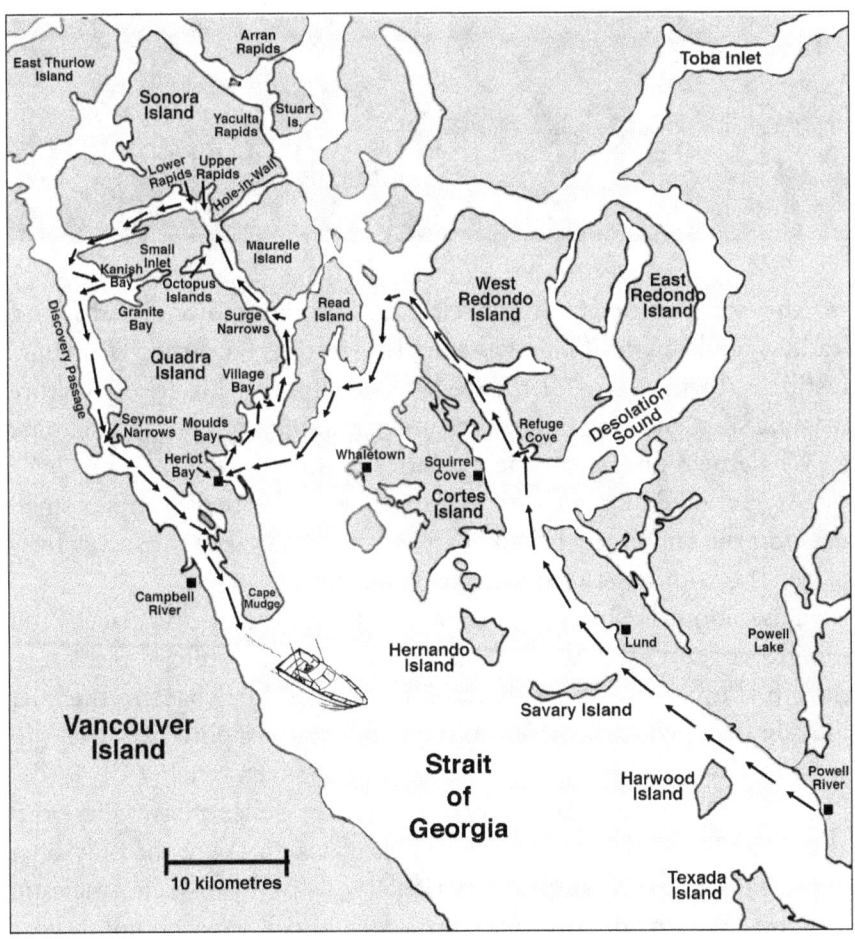

* * * * *

At the north end of Cortes, I select a route that crowds Read Island, leading us through Whale Passage. This setting (and the very name) instills historic visions of the peak of whaling in this area. I picture whaling ships plowing into this channel, chasing their prey, then home to Whaletown on the far side of Cortes Island.

At Heriot Bay, there's no waiting line at the fuel pump, a small dock on the end of the marina that seems too low-key for such a busy place. The young gas attendant helps us tie up.

I ask about business, and the boy tells me their dock space is full tonight, a good sign. While I pump the gas, my publicist goes up to the gift shop at the inn to check on book sales. She's back to the boat quickly (still plenty of copies on the shelf), and we push off and begin an idle-power cruise north, while we eat our snack lunch.

By 5 PM, we're secured for the night in Village Bay, where our anchor grabs on the first try in 30 feet of water. We're the only boat in the bay, a pleasant surprise, particularly since this is such a majestic location. My imagination goes into gear, and I see a booming First

Nations community on the shore (where it once was), with traditional "big houses" terraced on the gentle slope. The river pours in near where the natives resided, now tumbling noisily, its drop to the sea more pronounced by the low tide. I can't imagine a more perfect setting for a First Nations community.

That evening, on the Bayliner's aft deck, the Milky Way is visible early in the sparkling clear sky. As the night deepens, Jupiter rides low in the western sky, where the glow of Campbell River slightly interrupts the feeling of isolation. Overhead, the Summer Triangle (Vega, Deneb, and Altair) is perfectly centered on the zenith, where the Milky Way splits as it passes through Cygnus (the Northern Cross) and continues south in two streams. The branch to the left leads to Sagittarius and the center bulge of our galaxy, but tonight it's blocked by the light pollution of Campbell River (which, by the way, isn't the center of the universe).

The Big Dipper drops low this month, still riding well clear of the horizon after midnight in this high latitude. Here, the heavens are at least as dark as on Powell Lake, with the added benefit of being able to see more of the sky without the intervening mountains. The firmament seems enormous.

With my binoculars, I focus on the Andromeda Galaxy, the Milky Way's twin. In this secluded spot, on this dark night, Andromeda jumps out in the binoculars, spreading across nearly the full field of view. It's easy to discern the swirling shape of the on-angle disk, something that's not as easy to see in my high-quality amateur telescope. Low magnification and a corresponding wide field is the best way to view this amazing astronomical object. Sometimes you're just too close to the trees to see the forest.

I also inspect the Double Cluster in Perseus with my binoculars, a grand close gathering of stars. But this constellation's main claim to fame tonight is the Perseid meteor shower, an annual burst of shooting stars. Although I'm one day late in viewing the shower (it was cloudy at my cabin last night), tonight's meteors are better than almost any Perseid shower I've observed before (and I haven't missed many). The lack of moon tonight is a significant contributor to the high number of visible meteors, and this dark location adds to the ideal conditions. In past showers, I've seen Perseids streak brighter and with longer trails (although not in recent years), but the every-few-minutes pace of meteors tonight is fantastic.

I settle back in my canvas camp chair on the Bayliner's aft deck. The gentle breeze causes the boat to swing on anchor, drawing new constellations into view constantly. It's the perfect auto-observing position for a meteor shower, scanning the sky in slow, wide sweeps.

* * * * *

The next morning is a leisurely-paced departure. We'll need to leave Village Bay soon after 11:00, bringing us to Beazley Passage in Surge Narrows near low tide. I put my watch back on in preparation for the slack water event at 11:51.

We should start through the narrows a few minutes early, taking advantage of the last of the tide ebbing north, allowing those waiting on the other end of the passage to begin their transit south at the beginning of the flood. That way, we all get a slow push. Beazley isn't wide enough (comfortably) for big boats headed in opposite directions, and its swerves make it impossible to see all the way through the narrows to determine who is waiting on the other side. So common courtesy dictates that traffic heading north this morning enter the passage a few minutes before slack.

As we await our engine start time, Margy and I lounge on the aft deck, drinking coffee and watching Mitlenatch Island float in the distance, directly aligned with the entrance to Village Bay. "Float" isn't an unfitting term – Mitlenatch is disconnected from the ocean, another mirage of the island's many visual tricks. As it's native name implies, the double-hump of dark gray rock floats so-near yet so-far. This morning, the island seems only a few kilometres away. In fact, it "floats" 30 klicks to the south.

We prepare to raise anchor while listening to the FM radio's 11:00 local news and weather. The forecast promises more of the same cloudless skies for the rest of today, with good sea conditions through tomorrow afternoon.

By 11:15, we're cruising up Hoskyn Channel between Quadra and Read Island. We overtake three sailboats headed north, probably timing themselves for Beazley Passage. It's proof that the southward seasonal migration isn't yet in full swing.

With a few minutes to kill, we sit in position, perched near the dock at Surge Narrows. Meanwhile, two of the sailboats we passed move around us, hovering at the entrance to the passage. A runabout dashes between the islands to the west of Beazley Passage, headed north. It's not a recommended route for bigger boats, nor anyone less than expert, particularly at this low tide. But the runabout doesn't even slow down, and in a few minutes he's out of sight.

The first sailboat begins to move into the passage, and I maneuver the Bayliner to take up our position behind the second sailboat. The third boat we passed on our way up Hoskyn Channel is nowhere in sight, so we'll be the last to go through in this group. We wind into Beazley Passage in a mildly swirling flow, staying mid-channel through the majestic winding narrows.

Swinging around the main curve in the passage, I can now see three boats on the north end that are awaiting our exit. Once past the last obstacle, an underwater rock that shows clearly on our GPS, I maneuver to starboard to pass the sailboats in front of me. When the trawler waiting at the head of the southbound line sees me pull to the right, he quickly pushes forward into the passage. I check my watch – it's 11:47, officially four minutes before slack tide. This reminds me of a well-coordinated group of pilots taking off and landing at an uncontrolled airport. Air traffic control is unnecessary when everyone follows the accepted standards, and the flow of traffic is efficient and expeditious.

Our plan for today is loose, and I like it that way. The only timed hurdle involves Surge Narrows, and that's behind us. Now we cruise between Quadra and Maurelle Island. The tide has already turned at Hole in the Wall, so it will be too late to enter that passage before the current is too strong – or more precisely, too late to enter and have enough time to explore Hole in the Wall and exit by the same route. I'm not as sure about the two rapids at the corner of Quadra Island,

Upper and Lower Rapids. The tide tables indicate the flow in these waters can be significant, but my map depicts a wide channel that should be navigable well after slack. The only way to tell for sure is to take a look.

We pass the Octopus Islands, an alternate anchorage if the Upper or Lower Rapids is a problem. Based on the traffic I've seen so far on this trip, I'm not convinced that the southward migration of cruisers has passed yet, so I expect a busy anchorage in this popular spot. Like most beautiful bays on the south coast, I tend to avoid them and their summer crowds, in trade for less-traveled gunkholes. Of course, we're talking BC standards here – certainly there would be room in the Octopus Islands for our small Bayliner. But if we can make it to the other side of Quadra, I'm convinced Kanish Bay will be less populated.

As we cruise past Hole in the Wall, a powerboat is about to enter. The tide is now flooding (towards the northeast in this narrows), so we would not have time to make it in and back out comfortably. Without coming off-plane, Margy and I gaze back into Hole in the

Wall, catching a glimpse of the mountainous walls of the passage. It's pretty, but to Margy and me, our own paradise on Powell Lake can't be equaled by this more-famous landmark of the same name.

Ahead of us, Upper Rapids (which is below Lower Rapids when navigating in this direction) isn't severely roiling. Although swirls are brewing in the water, it seems docile.

"The current reminds me of Okeover," I say.

Like the current at Malaspina Inlet, just as you enter Okeover, it gets your attention, but it's nothing to worry about.

"Not a problem, so far," Margy agrees.

"Feel comfortable continuing through, to see what we find? We can always turn back and anchor in the Octopus Islands."

"Sure. It looks good to me."

Margy and I have a big advantage as a nautical crew. Similar to our tolerance of turbulence in light airplanes, our attitude towards the sea is similarly conservative. When it gets rough in either airplane or boat, we tend to declare our limits at nearly the same time. We may be wimps, but we make a good wimpy team. Since our personal limits are similar, we're never disappointed because one of us has decided to call it quits.

However, when it comes to tidal current (as opposed to the roughness of swells), I have the higher personal limit. Margy still remembers her first real current at Dodds Narrows in our kayak. It was the running of the rapids that thrilled me, but frightened her. It left an adverse impact that she's slowly, after several years, beginning to overcome. I see progress.

"We'll stay on-plane," I say. "The boat has better handling characteristics in mild current when traveling faster."

"Okay, that's fine."

And it is. We pass through Upper Rapids with barely a swerve in our path. The water is obviously disturbed, but far from threatening. Rounding the corner of Quadra Island, we enter Okosillo Channel and Lower Rapids. It's an easy transit, although we need to deviate around several lines of floatsam that are caught in troughs of the tidal flow. After the water settles down, we come off-plane, slowing to troll along the north side of Quadra Island.

This has been a good salmon year in Powell River. The Fish-o-Metre at Sam's shop has been consistently registering in the high "Moderate" region. Still, the salmon being caught are not nearly as plentiful as in past decades. The hint of improvement is encouraging. But here in Okisollo Channel, my coyote spoon and its flasher find nothing. I'm not a serious fisherman, but I do love to dabble in the sport in both fresh and salt water, and the majestic mountain background for relaxed fishing throughout coastal BC is superb. Except for one salmon I caught in Bute inlet, my record is terrible.

Kanish Bay, as expected, is relatively empty of boats. An oyster farm, spread in the back of the waterway, hinders our path to Granite Bay. We slow to near-idle, weaving our way through a loose assortment of blue and white floats. Granite Bay itself is lined with trailers, a sense of urbanity that I don't recall from my visit several years ago. There's room to anchor, but it doesn't feel comfortable. So we exit the bay and wind around the island near the entrance, and head towards Small Inlet.

I don't expect much, since this isn't a place I've read about, and the name makes me expect "tiny." But on the chart, the inlet extends far back into Quadra, where it nearly connects with the Octopus Islands.

The entrance to Small Inlet is wide but shallow (now near low tide), and I watch the bottom closely as we navigate inward. Then the water opens wide, and there only three boats anchored in this large basin. With plenty of room and a majestic setting, this is definitely our place for the night.

We stop outside the island near the head of the inlet. I use the Bayliner's catwalk to edge my way to the front deck. I lower our anchor into 15 feet of water, and Margy backs the Bayliner only a few metres. The hook grabs immediately.

"Two in a row!" Margy yells from the command bridge.

That's worth celebrating. For us, two successful drops in a row is much better than we expect.

As we swing gently on anchor, it's a gorgeous late afternoon on the aft deck. When the sun drops below the horizon, the sea calms even further, and the entrance to the inlet is reflected in the water in front of us.

Before calling it a night, Margy sets the alarm on her watch for 6 AM. This is a trip with an unusual amount of attention to the clock,

but necessary in regions where tidal flow is so strong. Slack tide at Seymour Narrows will be at 7:36, so the early alarm will allow us to navigate out of Small Inlet and Kanish Bay, and down the channel prior to high tide at the narrows.

Once again, we'll want to time our passage slightly before slack, to ride the rising tide south. In Seymour Narrows there's plenty of room to pass a boat headed in the opposite direction, but this route is best navigated within a few minutes of slack. And if you're late, you'll be even later on the other side of this lengthy passage. So I target 7:25 as the time to enter the narrows.

Our alarm is unnecessary. A few minutes before 6 o'clock, I'm awakened by a diesel engine starting nearby. The trawler anchored next to us probably has the same route in mind, but he needs to start earlier to make up for his slower speed.

We raise anchor, and Margy drives the Bayliner out of Small Inlet, passing through the entrance that's now considerably more comfortable at high tide. In fact, it seems almost exactly high tide here, even though it's still an hour until slack at Seymour Narrows. North of Campbell River, tides occur earlier, since the water floods in from the northern tip of Vancouver Island. Farther south, the flooding waters move in the opposite direction, flowing north from the Juan de Fuca Strait. However, in those southern areas (including Powell River), the delay in tidal flow is minimal, usually a matter of only a few minutes after Victoria. Here, nearer the northern end of Vancouver Island, the islands are more tightly packed, forming constrictions that delay the movement of tides and force it into swifter currents. There are exceptions, of course, such as Dodds Narrows and Porlier Pass to the south, but generally currents are more pronounced in the northern region.

As we exit Small Inlet, Margy brings the Bayliner onto plane, cruising straight through Kanish Bay, and then out into Discovery Passage. We pass a large fish trawler that seems to be sitting stationary near shore in the early morning shadow of Quadra Island. A huge wooden drum on the aft deck rotates slowly as it drops a net into the water.

While Margy drives, I follow our path on the GPS. In a wide bay to our right, several dozen small boats sit motionless. There's no dock nearby, nor any sign of buildings.

"Are they waiting to pass through Seymour Narrows?" asks Margy.

"No, that's still about 10 klicks. I guess they're fishing."

"Looks funny," replies Margy.

I nod my head in agreement. It does look strange. The boats are spaced almost perfectly distant from each other, none of them moving. Now one of the boats powers up and moves a few hundred metres north, then stops again.

"I'm sure these boats aren't waiting for slack tide at the narrows," I say. "This is too far north, and too many small boats."

"Maybe they came through Seymour Narrows just ahead of high tide, and that's a good fishing spot."

"Could be," I reply. "But they must have battled a pretty substantial current to get here. And it just doesn't look like a great fishing spot to me."

"Especially when you're surrounded by all those other boats," notes Margy.

It's true. Considering all of the beautiful places to fish in coastal BC, this isn't one of them. But Campbell River isn't far south from Seymour Narrows, and that city is known for sport fishing tours. This must be where they come to catch their salmon. It's not the kind of scenic fishing spot I imagined.

Although I profess otherwise, I'm not totally convinced this mass of boats is fishing rather than waiting for passage through Seymour Narrows. It's a long ways from the pass, and there are too many small vessels to fit the criteria for a line of waiting boats. Still, although I tell Margy I'm certain these boats don't mark the place to wait for slack tide passage, I'm a bit apprehensive. When the water remains calm for more several kilometres, I'm finally confident of our decision to press on. I show Margy our location on the GPS, and she continues on-plane towards Seymour Narrows.

"Is it too early?" she asks.

"All seems calm, so I say let's go, even though it's twenty minutes before slack."

"I'll slow if the water starts to swirl too much," she answers.

I'm pleased she's still in command of *Halcyon Days*, not asking me to take the helm for our passage through the narrows. She continues right on through, following well behind a tug that's towing a large barge. The water remains amazingly calm, with a few swirls to the sides, but nothing of concern.

Once we clear the promontory that marks the end of the narrows, the water gets a little rough. We're entering the area where the flow is beginning to reverse, flowing out to the north. Margy maneuvers around the barge and its tug, crossing waves that come every which way. I was most concerned about the area now behind us, but now it's a struggle all the way to April Point. Traffic in the channel doesn't help, with wakes of large boats mixing with the churning tidal flow.

I try calling April Point Marina on VHF, but there's no answer. It's now a few minutes before 8:00, so probably no one is in the office yet. We motor past the resort's empty sport fishing dock and the lodge office, headed towards the marina.

We find several open spots at the docks. An end spot seems appropriate, since it's only big enough for us and won't block any incoming large vessels. We tie-up there, leaving a note: "Gone to breakfast at the lodge. Back by 9:00."

When we walk up the ramp to shore, the marina office door is open. The young woman there is talking on the telephone, with a VHF microphone dangling in the other hand. She has probably just arrived at work on what will be a busy summer day. When she hangs up, I try to get her attention before she attends to the VHF radio.

"We parked on the end of 'E' Dock," I say quickly, knowing she has business to attend to. "Is that okay, while we go to breakfast?"

"Perfect," she says in a relaxed manner, replacing the microphone in its cradle. "No shore power there anyway, so we can't rent the spot."

"Is there a fee?" I ask.

"No problem," she replies. "Enjoy your breakfast."

We do.

* * * * *

On the next leg, now headed home, I drive. We slowly motor out of the marina, past the still-empty sport fishing dock.

"Seems funny there aren't any boats at that dock," I say.

"Not so strange when you realize where they are," replies Margy. "Up at dawn, through Seymour Narrows before the change of tides, and in position for fishing by slack tide."

"High slack is supposed to be a good time for salmon," I say. "So that explains where all of those small fishing boats came from."

Rather than increase engine power when we clear the point, I continue at idle so we can listen to the radio. As we're propelled slowly south along the shore towards Cape Mudge, we wait for the long-range weather forecast on a local FM channel. Meanwhile, the water continues to roil, well over an hour after high tide.

Across the channel near the sport fisherman hotel, Painters Lodge, a bright orange seaplane begins its takeoff roll. The throaty roar of the Beaver on floats is an attention-getting sound.

"Look, there's another one behind it," says Margy.

Right behind the orange seaplane is a blue-and-white floatplane, another Beaver, lined up for takeoff.

"And another!" says Margy.

Sure enough, as soon as the second seaplane is airborne, another orange Beaver takes its place in the takeoff line. It's as if these floatplanes are generating from nothing.

Every other airplane taking its position in line is orange, probably representing a charter operation. Alternating blue-and-white and orange seaplanes take to the skies only a few minutes apart, banking towards the north as soon as they're airborne. This continues until five airplanes are in the air in only a few minutes.

It feels more civilized here, floating only a kilometre from Campbell River, although I'm not convinced that's a good thing. Not all bad, but not all good either. Floatplanes are part of the British Columbian experience. Maybe they're carrying fisherman even farther north than that touristy-looking fishing cove just north of Seymour Narrows.

"Welcome back to civilization," I say.

But I really wish we weren't.

Chapter 3

Okeover

I awaken to a bright spread of light in the Bayliner's V-berth. The alarm hasn't yet gone off, so it must be before 6 am. I stretch my feet out the narrow opening in the center of the berth's entry area, which aggravates a kink in my right shoulder blade. This thin mattress, covered by a light sleeping bag, feels good on my back. I sleep well in this confined space. But after two days, I begin to feel the thick plywood foundation below the mattress. It's a small price to pay for a good night's sleep.

I glance at my watch (6:30!), and immediately begin to clamber out of the V-berth.

"You slept through the alarm," says Margy, already awake and providing the answer to my question. "But I didn't think it was important."

Sleeping through noise, even a faint beep like this one, isn't like me. I must have been even more comfortable than I thought.

"No problem. But let's get going before the tide drops much lower."

Low tide isn't until 11:06, but the water is already coming down fast. This tide will be a low-low, and I want to get out of here soon. We're once again anchored in one of my all-time favourite spots in this world – behind the peninsula (almost an islet) near the entry to Theodosia Inlet. The narrow connection to Lancelot Inlet is nearly a river, navigable at low tide, but I'd prefer lots of water.

On the aft deck, everything is wet. I didn't hear rain during the night. Then again, I didn't hear the alarm either. It's one of those June mornings when the temperature has dropped to the dewpoint. You can feel the moisture in the air. It always feels so thick, yet moist air is actually thinner than dry, since the water vapor displaces air. You'd believe that if you ever try to takeoff in a small airplane, like my Piper Arrow, on a hot day with high humidity.

There's no need to secure everything for this brief trip to Okeover, but I put away a few loose items. I pull the satellite radio antenna off the foredeck, retracting it through the hatch above the V-berth. Then I tidy up the cabin. Things can fly around, even in smooth water.

Margy sits at the helm on the command bridge, ready to keep the Bayliner in position while I raise the anchor. The hook comes up caked in black mud, so I motion to Margy to start out of the bay while I lower the anchor again and pull it out of the water with a shake. It cleans itself nicely, so I haul it aboard and stow it against the metal bracket. I leave the rode and chain loose on the deck, awaiting our planned stop at Okeover. Then I maneuver around the cabin on the catwalk and climb to the command bridge to join Margy.

"You mind if I drive?" I ask.

Margy says nothing, but I know she concurs. She slips out of the bench seat driving position, and I slide in. The "river" connection to Lancelot can be challenging to amateur boaters like us. I power-up a bit, still plowing a lot of water.

"The blue workboat is coming in," she says.

I watch the sleek blue-and-silver crew boat sweep in front of us, headed towards the logging dock. I've seen this particular boat in Theodosia many times. This is why I want to drive this morning. It's time for the loggers to come to work, and I doubt the workboat captain is planning to take it slow. The goal is to get everyone to their trucks and on-the-job quickly. Time is money, and a recreational boat in the middle of the channel between Theodosia and Lancelot would be worth a few choice words.

"Keep an eye on him," I state. "Let me know if he makes a quick drop-off at the dock for another trip."

Margy swings around to watch the crew boat. I push the throttle forward a little more, to speed our progress toward the channel. I watch for other boats coming around the corner from Lancelot Inlet, too, since the blue boat isn't the only workboat here. Based on the short time between runs yesterday, I assume the Okeover wharf is where the boats gather their logging crews.

"He's coming out again," announces Margy.

I judge the distance to the channel and decide to wait for the blue boat. I pull over to the shore near the peninsula. Good decision – the boat is upon us in a matter of seconds. He blasts to our left and then turns sharply to enter the channel at full-cruise. I wave but can't see whether my greeting is returned from the enclosed cabin. But I bet this fancy maneuver is for our benefit! This is a repeat of a repeat, now becoming a regular ritual. If I were the captain, I'd do the same thing every time I saw our Bayliner, while shaking my fist and yelling "Tourons!"

Now I can slip back into the center of the channel and make the snaking turn out of Theodosia. Once in Lancelot Inlet, I come up on-plane and cruise down the center of the fjord-like inlet, dodging a few prawn balls. These scotchmen are dark gray, rather than the traditional orange, so maybe they shouldn't even be called "scotchmen."

Approaching the junction of Lancelot and Okeover Inlet, I notice Margy has the Canadian Hydrographic Service chart on her lap: "Watch out for the rock just off the penninsula," she says.

The rock beyond Edith Island sticks up as a warning at this decreasing tide, though it's barely awash at high tide. It's the worst kind of obstacle, more easily visible at low water than high. Imagine passing over it when the rock is barely submerged – scrape, thud, crash!

"Which way?" asks Margy.

As usual, our plans are flexible. We've discussed lunch at the Laughing Oyster, near the Okeover wharf, but we've also talked about anchoring at Grace Harbour until lunch-time. Or should we tie up at the wharf now and explore the shore?

I glance at the surrounding clouds, notice a few bright patches to the west, and point to the right: "Grace Harbour."

We round Scott Point and the mansion-like cabin on the tip. Passing a wide harbour with a few small cabins, we slow to near-idle for entry to Grace Harbour.

It's my first time into this anchorage, and I'm surprised by the feeling of remoteness. I expected more homes visible from inside the harbour. But, except for a few cabins near the entrance, it's a tranquil spot. Of course, off-season boating makes a big difference in the feel of any place.

As we approach the narrowing channel that leads into the harbour, a large sailboat seems parked right in the middle of the entry. It's pointed directly at us, sail stowed.

"Does it look like he's under power?" I ask Margy.

"I think so," she replies. "Hard to tell."

"Must be. Otherwise, he's sitting right in the middle of the channel."

As we approach closer, I can see no wake spreading from the bow, so I conclude he's stopped. Then I notice a man standing near the stern, adjusting the towing line for his dinghy.

"I think he's just getting underway," I note. "Big sailboats have a large keel, so he needs the center of the channel."

The boat slowly begins to move forward, out of the narrow passage. As the sailboat exits, we slip behind and straight through.

Near the back of the bay, five sailboats are anchored in a single group, probably traveling together. An additional two boats occupy the forward section of the anchorage. That leaves plenty of room for us.

The extreme back end of the bay is open. In mid-summer, there would be several boats anchored here on stern lines, but today this area is vacant.

We drop anchor in 30-feet of water. As I monitor the rode on the forward deck, Margy backs the Bayliner to set the hook,. The line comes almost taunt, but not quite snug, and the anchor begins to drag. I grab the extended rode with my hand and feel the intermittent thump of the bottom. But it's good enough for a brief stop in no-wind conditions, so I motion to Margy to cut the engine.

We settle into a morning of relaxed preparation for our return to Powell River. It's better than blasting straight home. I call it decompression time – easing our way back into society after several sequestered days swinging on the hook.

I stow items we won't need again on this trip. Then I settle in with a science fiction book that features FTL (faster-than-light) transport. Here I am at a slower-than-society place, reading about FTL.

* * * * *

As noon approaches, I raise the anchor for the short trip to the Okeover wharf. Before stowing the chain and rode, I lean over the bow and take a last look at the numerous jellyfish that inhabit Grace Harbour. These waters are famous for the plethora of non-stinging jellyfish (my favourite kind). Today they pump their Saturn-like rings in a pulsing motion right near the surface. Maybe it's related to the tide that's now near its lowest ebb. Jellyfish ride the slack tide and seem to take particular joy in the special occasion.

Outbound from the anchorage, just inside the narrow channel, two kayaks and a canoe slip quietly by us. They may be part of the five-boat gathering, out for a morning paddle. In the widening passage, gentle, wide swirls of water appear all around us as herring jump and plop down in their demonstration of carefree belly flops. Low tide tends to bring out the best in nature.

After exiting Grace Harbour, the exposed rocks to our left near Scott Point are now so large in the low tide that it takes on the appearance of a true island. Seagulls are congregated there now. They'll have a few hours to sun themselves before the island transforms itself back into an invisible obstacle to navigation.

We travel along the shore of Coode Peninsula at slow cruise to minimize our wake, while absorbing the sights. The route passes white-and-blue lines of floating balls that mark the numerous oyster farms. Nowhere will you find more densely-packed oyster farms than in Okeover Inlet. Lately, Powell River's newspaper has been sporting editorials about the on-and-off battle between supporters and opponents of these leased waters. It's locally called the Oyster Wars.

I remember the pride I felt when I picked up a menu in a popular San Diego seafood restaurant to find "Desolation Sound Oysters" as a featured appetizer. Of course, I ordered them, and they were excellent. In my imagination, I pictured oysters traveling south from one of these bays right here in Okeyover. I'm on the side of the supporters.

Three kayaks, two of them doubles, paddle near the shore of Coode Peninsula. They are probably from Powell River Sea Kayak's bay at the south end. They're headed out against a slowly rising tide, but the wind is behind them. Their paddles make windmill-like circular strokes against the gray-green background of the choppy water.

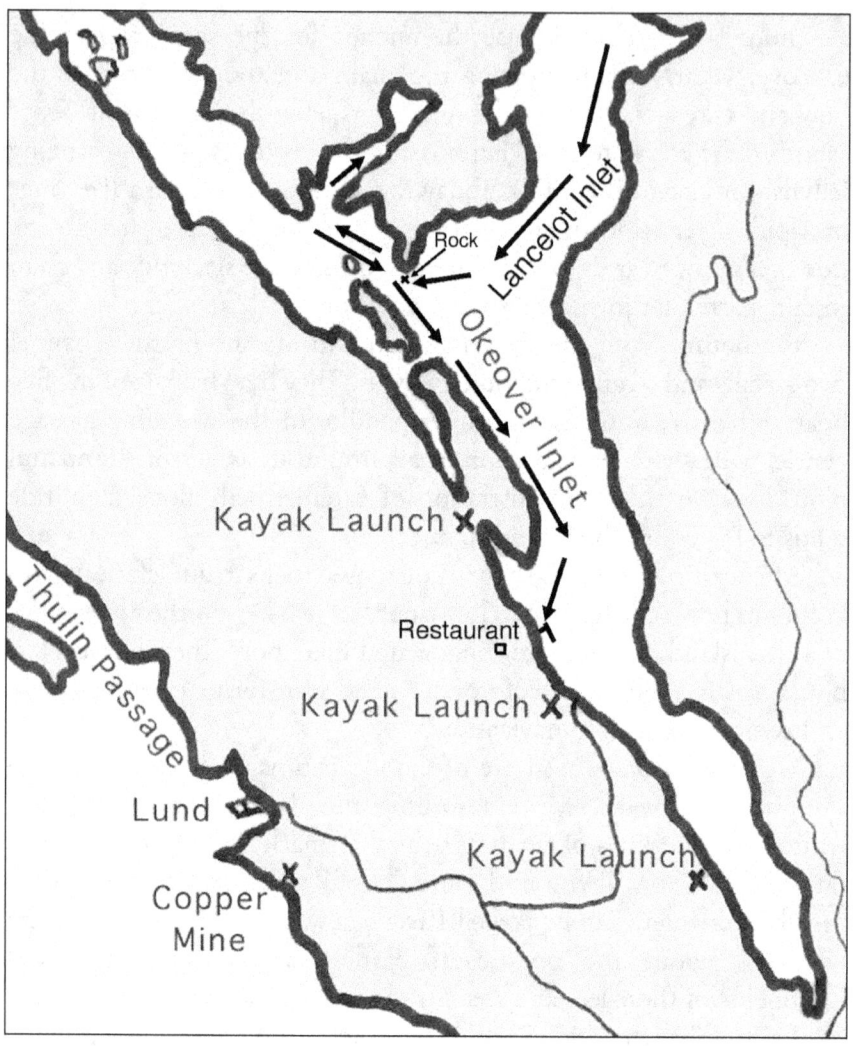

After clearing the peninsula, I power up, but the bow is sluggish coming on-plane. I push the dual trim tab switches to their full travel, seeking a full bow-down configuration as we accelerate. But still we plow through the water.

"Bow's up," says Margy.

"What?"

I don't understand. I have the trim switches all the way back, so that should keep the bow down so we can properly accelerate. "Oh!" I'm caught again by the difference between this boat and the Campion

I use more often. Pushing back on the trim switches in this boat is "bow up." No wonder we aren't accelerating. I push the twin switches forward, and the boat begins to accelerate nicely. Within a few seconds, we're on-plane.

Several spots are vacant at the Okeover dock,. The workboats at Theodosia will be gone until early evening, so this is the time to find dock space. Of course, docking real estate is more available in June than in the busier months of July and August.

The entry to the wharf is clearly marked, with both a triangular red marker to our right and a square green sign to the left. Red-right-returning: you can't go wrong here. The wind is pushing towards the north, and this will be a bit of a challenge. Even clearing the entry takes concentration, to prevent drifting towards the red marker.

Inside the log breakwater, the best parking spot is obvious. It sits at the end of the front dock finger. A small metal boat is docked to the south of this open area, it's large 4-stroke Honda sticking out towards the empty spot. I'm not sure which way to make my approach, particularly with the outboard motor protruding towards the empty spot.

"I'll dock on the right side," I yell down to Margy.

She's already positioned on the port side of the aft deck. She has guessed I'll dock there, since that's normally my preferred side. The ropes are always ready on the left side, although the right side is easily prepared for an arrival.

I notice that Margy pushes the deck chairs to the left side, as she prepares for docking on the right. As I turn the boat for the arrival, I begin to drift faster than expected.

"I've changed my mind," I yell down to Margy on the aft deck. "It'll be the left side."

I see Margy out the corner of my eye, as she scurries to the other side, pushing the chairs out of the way again. I turn the boat and start to back into the open spot, but the drift pushes me out of position again. I give in to what is happening, gun the engine a bit, swing the wheel to its full limit, and point the boat out of the confined area. I'll circle around for another try.

"Back on the right side, after all," I proclaim.

Chairs shift, ropes fly, and finally all is working out just right. I slip into the spot, a respectable (and safe) 2 metres behind the protruding Honda outboard. The Bayliner barely taps the dock in a near-perfect arrival. The third time is a charm.

As we secure the boat for our walk to the Laughing Oyster, I watch a woman in dull yellow khakis and a light-blue windbreaker. She releases a large plastic box from the top of the pier, down the steeply-inclined wooden walkway. The box zooms down the planks and slides out onto the dock. Then she does the same with another box. I watch her lift a moderate-size propane tank, and it looks like she briefly considers the same route (I hope not!). Then she carries the tank down the ramp, a particular steep descent at low tide. She promptly loads the boxes and tank into a skookum, welded-aluminum boat with a big unmarked gray outboard. Then she deftly unties her lines, while simultaneously reaching inside the boat to hit the starter. She hops aboard and…

I expect her to promptly motor out of the breakwater entrance. Instead, she points the bow to the inside line of the breakwater logs and slips out the side of the wharf, only a few metres from the beach. The water is obviously deep enough at low tide to handle a boat, but I would never have guessed it.

"Looks like she knows what she's doing," I say to Margy.

"Sure does. Quick and efficient, but it scared me."

"Makes my docking look like an amateur."

Before walking the road to the restaurant, a boat with "Park Ranger" in bright blue markings demands a visit. It's a 26-foot powerboat with a sturdy inflated dinghy that rocks gently from a large A-frame crane on the stern.

"Looks official," I note.

Sometimes, recreational boaters imitate the markings of government boats, such as old forestry boats.

"Desolation Sound is a marine park, you know, so maybe that's the park ranger," replies Margy. "Nice boat."

* * * * *

Lunch at the Laughing Oyster is excellent, as it always is. As for oysters, this is the place, a lot closer to the food source than San Diego.

The restaurant is completely empty when we enter at 12:45 on a Friday, probably not to be repeated once the real summer begins. We sit on the outside deck, overlooking the wharf. The Bayliner looks stately, parked among the working boats of the region.

Gazing down on the wharf, I watch two white single-seat kayaks paddling north, just outside the breakwater. They're probably from Y-Knot, a small resort near the head of Okeover. The wind has now dissipated, so they are facing a rising tide without wind assist. But, if they time things right, they'll have an easy ride home on the flooding tide.

The dark blue crew boat from Theodosia appears on the horizon, blasting towards the wharf. Its spreading wake indicates a straight path from Lancelot Inlet. There's no wasted time for these boats. The boat slows as it approaches the wharf, but slides around the side. Like the woman in khakis, this saves a few minutes. The large boat slips between the beach and the inner log of the breakwater. Time is money.

With its dual engines still running, the boat drops two passengers in bright orange vests, both carrying a large chainsaw. Then the blue boat quickly departs the same way it came, slipping out along the beachside route. Work goes on in the heart of Theodosia.

* * * * *

Outbound from the wharf, we pass the two white kayaks abeam the peninsula. Because of our substantial wake, we give them a wide berth.

As we prepare to exit Okeover Inlet, the final narrow passage between the island (nearly a peninsula) and the opposite shore approaches. Now, at mid-tide, the water churns in a whirling roiled appearance. It's far from threatening. Instead, it adds to the tranquility of this place.

Departing Okeover, I power up and round Sarah Point. Beyond the promontory, the water is a bit rough, although not enough to be of concern. Nevertheless, the inside route through Thulin Passage will be smoother today, so I aim the Bayliner at the Copeland Islands. There are no boats in sight and none are likely in the island anchorages today. So we may not need to reduce to no-wake speed.

We slip past Bliss Landing and into the passage. Even at the popular marine park anchorage near the center of the Copelands, there are no boats. So we motor on through on-plane.

At Lund, we're the only boat at the fuel dock – another sign that mid-June isn't yet true summer. The fuel dock is still operating under limited winter hours.

I climb the ramp to the hotel and pop in for a quick visit to Tug-Ghum Gallery, to check the status of my books sold there. At the front counter, Debra sits at-work on a polished, stone rendition of a seal popping its head out of the water. Debra's artistry is amazing. I carry one of her hand-made postcards in my backpack. It's a skillful interpretation of a cutthroat trout hitting an underwater lure in Powell Lake. It's one of my favourite drawings to share with friends.

The good news is Debra has only one copy of *Up the Lake* remaining on the shelf, and it's not even summer. So we arrange for more books.

*****

On the final leg home, we pass just to the outside of the Atrevida buoy that marks the shallow water closer to shore. Mildly-threatening clouds ride over Texada Island and to the left, over the Powell Lake area. These two dark patches are undoubtedly producing rain.

A few kilometres later, a refreshing cool blast of air pushes out from the storm to our left. We ride towards home, just out front of this mini-tempest, not feeling a drop of rain.

We pass between the Harwood spit and a huge boom of logs being towed south. The tug is a large low-stern vessel, one of the bigger tugs of the strait. We cruise past, only about 100 feet to the side, and I wave at the tugboat captain from our command bridge. I wonder if he's waving back from inside his cabin. Is his trek south just another job in these enchanting waters? Could he be bored with the passing scenery?

The tall smokestack of the paper mill is to our left, now idle after years of proclaiming the kraft mill's dominance over the waterfront. Shafts of sunlight beam down on the floating hulks of the company's breakwater. The pier of Willingdon Beach is visible only a few kilometres ahead under a patch of black. I sight the high rock breakwater of Westview's North Harbour. We safely ride home on the leading edge of the small storm.

Chapter 4

Mr. Buttercup

Ken has talked about going to Alaska for years, and I'm certain he's destined to make the trip. In fact, when I first met him, it looked like he was going to try it in his 17-foot welded aluminum Silver Streak. His wife, Sam (Samantha), has traveled with Ken on a variety of up-coast adventures, but long distance travel in the Silver Streak is really roughing it (*Up the Strait*, Chapter 7). Ken has convinced me that I'll want to make the trip someday, too, but I'm not sure I would feel comfortable launching for Alaska in my 24-foot Bayliner, as elaborate as it is in comparison to the Silver Streak.

When I receive Ken's email, it catches me by surprise. Ken and Sam have decided to buy a bigger boat, an Eaglecraft Outlaw 28-footer with twin outboards. They've contracted for a brand-new boat, to be built to their specifications in Campbell River. Ken refers to the Silver Streak as "practical" and to the Outlaw as "wild and crazy."

"You can buy a condo for the price of this boat, but we don't need a condo, so there you go," says Ken.

My first greedy thoughts involve an opportunity to take our Bayliner to Alaska, following in the protective footsteps of this bigger boat. But Ken can't wait for me. He and Sam are already scheduled to depart in a few months, part of a group who purchased their boats from the same Campbell River manufacturer. Their plan is to speed up the coast in only three days, tour Alaska more leisurely, and then charge back home. I'm not ready for such a trip this year, but maybe Ken can iron out the kinks of the route this summer, and I can tag along on a repeat (hopefully slower) cruise next year.

Nearly every week, Ken and Sam travel north from their home in Gibsons to check on the construction status of their new boat. That takes them through Powell River, to take the ferry to Comox, and

Margy and I plan to meet them for breakfast. But when we walk into the cafe, Ken is missing.

"He's across the street at the marine shop," says Sam. "He can't pass a boat store without stopping."

I leave Margy and Sam in the cafe, and walk across the street. Just as I reach the store, Ken is walking out of Marine Traders.

"Always looking for a bargain," he says.

"Have you been to the showroom next door?" I ask

"What showroom?"

That does it for the next hour. I introduce Ken to the boat dealer as "my friend who's going to Alaska." We walk through cramped aisles of outboard motors, chain saws, motorcycles, and dinghies. Then we climb the stairs to the upper floor where the bigger equipment displays are almost hidden from the store below. It's my favourite kind of showroom – no salesmen in sight. Ken and I wander through the upstairs hangar-sized room, where a mix of new boats and quads are on display.

Finally we make it back to the cafe, in time for a quick breakfast before Sam and Ken must board the ferry. They are regulars on this route, more often than expected when the progress on construction of their boat begins to slip. Production delays are not unexpected on such a major boat-building project, but it's starting to impact their scheduled departure for Alaska.

Ken has decided to register the boat, a process a bit more demanding than simply licensing it. But when Ken decides he wants to do something, regardless of the advice of others, he's going to do it. The exterior colour selected for the boat's cabin is yellow, so the name *Buttercup* is selected, but there's already another Canadian boat with that registered name, so it can't be used.

"You'll like our final suggestion," says Sam. "We searched and searched for a variation on the theme of *Buttercup*, and finally we found one that wasn't registered."

"*Mister Buttercup?*" I say.

Sam knows I've designated *Mister* names for nearly everything I own.

"Right!" exclaims Sam. "I thought you'd like it."

Actually, I feel quite honoured, as if I have a part in this project. But I'm also concerned that *Mr. Buttercup's* sea trials are going to have to be uncomfortably accelerated to allow Ken and Sam to join the group headed north to Alaska.

"Once we get the boat in the water, we'll need some break-in time mighty fast," says Ken. "It's important to get at least 20 hours on the boat before we head north, so we can get the first major maintenance check before we leave. The first few hours will be in Campbell River, learning to drive."

He says this with a touch of intimidation. Moving up to a boat this size from my Bayliner would be a significant step. For Ken, it's an even bigger leap. It'll be a sturdy, reliable boat for almost any conditions, and a huge move up from his Silver Streak.

Mr. Buttercup creeps towards its much-delayed launch and sea trials, sitting proudly at the boat factory. I admire the crew boat shape, my favourite design.

I formulate a plan to assist Ken and Sam with the logistics of the boat delivery process, and it will give Margy and me a chance to be more involved in the project. I propose that we assist with their ground transportation, since they'll be taking delivery of the boat in Campbell River. As part of the engine break-in, Ken suggests that he pick us up in *Mr. Buttercup* at Powell River. Then we'll return with him to Campbell River where we can assist by driving their car back to Powell River. Although I volunteer Margy and me for the car trip, I secretly hope I can get more time in the boat if Sam and Margy drive back in the car.

Another part of Ken's break-in plan is to join up with the Gibsons Yacht Club on their annual voyage to Desolation Sound. Both *Mr. Buttercup* and our Bayliner (which we seldom refer to as *Halcyon Days*, although it's a fine name) can zip ahead of the other Gibsonites or follow later, since our higher speed doesn't match the slower sailboats in the group.

* * * * *

It comes right down to the wire. Ken and Sam are in Campbell River when the Gibsons Yacht Club is scheduled to arrive in Powell River. The new boat is now in the water, but I still await Ken's "We're ready" telephone call. Meanwhile, a series of stormy days has left the yacht club behind schedule, sheltered in Secret Cove to the south. From our condo patio, I look out over Westview Harbour towards an ominously white-capped chuck.

I dial Ken's cell phone, and hear it connect. Then I hear a voice in the background, and it sounds like Ken's.

"*Daisy*, this is *Buttercup*. How do you hear?"

It's clearly Ken's voice, but who is he talking to?

"This is *Daisy*," answers a female voice in the background. "You're loud and clear."

"Did you just dial me on the phone?" asks Ken, in a voice distant from the phone.

"No, that wasn't me," replies a dim, scratchy voice I don't recognize. I've obviously interrupted a radio call.

"Okay, *Buttercup* out," says Ken.

I expect him to pick up the phone now, but he doesn't. I hear Ken moving around in his boat, with wind or wave noises in the background.

"Hey, *Mister Buttercup*, this is *Mister Float Cabin*!" I yell my message into the phone, trying to get Ken's attention.

Nothing.

"Answer the phone!" I yell.

Still nothing.

Finally I hang up, wait a few minutes and dial again. Ken answers on the second ring.

"*Mister Buttercup* in Campbell River, this is *Mister Float Cabin* in Powell River," I say, this time in a normal conversational tone.

"Hey *Mister Float Cabin*. So that was you calling."

"T'was me, Ken. Who is *Daisy*?"

"Oh, that's Sam, back in the hotel room. She's reorganizing."

He says the word "reorganizing" with a slow, critical tone, implying they are accumulating a lot of things, and there's lots of packing going on. Ken and Sam have been hauling boat equipment from Gibsons for weeks, and I wonder how it will all fit into the new boat.

"How are the sea trials going?" I ask.

"Sea trials are finished. Now it's my own docking trials, and I'm not doing very good. This boat is a lot to handle during docking."

"With two engines, you should be able to maneuver into almost any spot," I say, adding: "Once you get the hang of it."

"That's the problem," laughs Ken. "So far, I haven't got the hang of it."

"I'm sure the weather isn't helping," I suggest. "The swells are pretty big here, although things are starting to settle down after yesterday."

"Not bad here," he says. "But my docking definitely needs work. We won't be going to Powell River today."

I look across the chuck, towards Campbell River. I can't see that far, with Harwood Island in the way, but I extrapolate what I see in the clouds overhead. There's more blue sky in his direction than mine.

"Well, when you get here, the fuel dock is a nice open area," I offer as encouragement. "Not much to whack into."

"I know. It's a good dock, but I'm not ready to try it yet. Besides, it's probably pretty rough mid-strait today."

"Sure, we'll be ready when you are," I remind him. "Just let me know when you're coming. I'll clear out everybody near the fuel dock. I'll just yell out: 'Here comes Ken!' That should do it."

"Thanks, I needed that."

*****

As is common when I have a few extra days (or even hours), I head back up the lake. There's no sense cooling my heels in town when I could be at my float cabin.

I've checked on the Gibsons Yacht Club again by phoning the wharfinger at Westview Harbour.

"Nobody from Gibsons has registered yet," says Jim.

That puts them at least a full day behind schedule. They're delayed by the weather, Ken is delayed by the weather, and I'm cozy at my cabin.

That evening I call Ken to see how his docking practice is proceeding.

"Better," says Ken. "On the second try today, I did pretty well. But those twin-throttles are a handful."

"But wait until you get used to them," I counter. "With two engines, you'll be able to spin around on a dime, and dock like you have a bow thruster."

"That's then, not now," says Ken.

He's a perpetual optimist, but not when it comes to these new throttles.

"So do you think you're coming across tomorrow?"

"Maybe," says Ken. "Sam and I need to discuss some things with the boat builder tomorrow morning, and let's see what happens with the weather."

"I'll be ready. What do you hear from the yacht club?"

"They should be in Powell River tomorrow, except for Klaus and Fran. They're still back at Gibsons, with an oil leak, so the club will probably wait for them in Powell River."

"So the club will be in town at least one night?"

"Probably two. It'll take Klaus a while to catch up in the Uniflite."

The 31-foot Uniflite has been modified with two fuel-efficient small diesels, traveling trawler-like. Klaus' problems have bought us some extra time.

* * * * *

A voicemail message from Sam the next morning is a surprise: "Change of plans – again. Campbell River is calm, and Ken plans to go for it while he has a chance. I'm driving the car to Powell River, taking the 3:15 PM ferry from Comox. If the weather doesn't cooperate, Ken will follow the ferry. Hope to see you in Powell River."

Sam sounds like she feels there are too many loose ends. Sheltered water lies behind a big ferry like the *Queen of Burnaby*. Smaller boats sometimes take advantage of the protected wake in major swells. Ken could travel south from Campbell River to Comox, then follow the ferry across to Powell River. If the weather is acceptable, he'll come across before the ferry, arriving in Powell River as early as 2 o'clock. Good plan. I call Ken to confirm things.

"Hello, *Mister Buttercup*. This is *Mister Float Cabin*."

Ken is at the dock in Campbell River, preparing for the trip across the strait. His voice has a sense of confidence, mixed with an occasional crackle of concern."

"Can you meet me at the fuel barge to help me dock?"

"Of course," I reply. "It'll take me a little while to pack up here and come back down the lake. But I'll beat you to the fuel dock."

"Warn the wharfinger that a beginner is arriving in a thirty-foot boat and needs a wide and easy boat slip for overnight."

The word "warn" sticks in my mind. Ken is about to launch for Alaska, and he's still struggling with routine docking in *Mr. Buttercup*. Plus, he readily admits he has never anchored in his Silver Streak, which is logical (once I think it through) considering the small boat's lack of overnight accommodations.

"You've grown," I reply. "Are you a twenty-eight-foot boat or a thirty-footer?"

"Technically, twenty-eight. But thirty with the outboards sticking out."

"Call me when you start across," I say before hanging up. "I'll be at the gas dock to grab you."

"Bring plenty of help," says Ken.

* * * * *

Margy is in the middle of cooking late-morning sourdough pancakes when I tell her Ken is coming. I hurry her along (only so fast for pancakes) so we can eat our breakfast, pack up, and travel down the lake.

The first few kilometres of our trip finds calm water under drizzly skies. Then, near Three-Mile Bay, the water roils a bit, as gusts kick around the lower lake. The Campion's bow slaps the waves, splashing water over the windshield. By the time we dock at the Shinglemill, near noon, whitecaps are everywhere on this end of the lake.

"I hope Ken follows the ferry," says Margy, as we pull into our parking slip.

Clear the waters of British Columbia – here comes Ken!

* * * * *

From our condo in town, I call Ken's cell phone. He answers but the connection is bad. He shouts into the phone ("Hello! Hello!"), with lots of background noise that sounds like the engine coupled with – I have an active imagination – the crashing of waves. The call ends abruptly, as I hear a terminating disconnect: *Click*!

I try again, and this time the connection is better, but I still hear the disturbing background noise. Ken is in a hurry to finish the call.

"I'm near Mitlenatch. Pretty bad here. Gotta' go!"

"I'll try calling you from the Bayliner," I offer. "What frequency?"

"Channel sixty-nine!" he yells over the sound of the background noise.

Ken hangs up abruptly, leaving me with an open, gaping mouth that no one sees. My first thought is that Ken is in over his head – a concept I immediately realize is a poor choice of words. He's coming almost directly across the Strait of Georgia, rather than following the ferry. Ken has considerable experience in rough water in his smaller Silver Streak, so these must be hefty swells. Knowing Ken like I do, he may be facing a major challenge at the moment, but he's retaining his positive attitude. In fact, I bet he's enjoying the challenge of pounding through the waves. He's probably grinning at this very moment. At least a little.

*****

From Westview's North Harbour, I call Ken on the radio, using the Bayliner's VHF: "*Buttercup, Buttercup*, this is *Halcyon Days* on Channel six-nine."

"*Halcyon Days*, hello!" replies Ken. "Things are a lot better now, near Hernando Island. I'm going to circle around to get on the downwind side."

"Roger, *Buttercup*. It's better here too."

I know the route from Hernando south, and Ken should find better-protected waters for the rest of his trip.

"Thanks, *Halcyon Days*. Did you find me a good slip?"

"How does a 100-foot berth sound?"

"Right now it sounds pretty good. Bring lots of help."

Since this is the second time he's asked, I'd better find what he wants.

*****

I haven't arranged a 100-foot slip for Ken. In fact, in the race of recent events, I haven't even contacted the wharfinger. At Powell River, that would normally be a problem, since parking for transient vessels is so limited. But somehow Jim always finds a way, even if it means rafting boats together.

I visit Jim (known as "Buzz" to many of his friends) in his wooden shack, perched temporarily on cement blocks near the excavation for the new waterfront project. As I climb the creaky stairs, a visiting boater is just leaving the tiny office. I back away from the door to let him out. It's difficult to imagine fitting three people in this small room simultaneously.

"Is the Gibsons Yacht Club here?" I ask.

"Arrived last night," says Jim. "I had to spread them out a bit, but they are down there." He motions towards the South Harbour, now partly out of sight below us in this low tide.

"Room for one more?"

"Always," replies Jim. "How big?"

"Thirty feet, but he needs an easy spot. Brand new boat – been in the water only a few days – and this guy drives worse than me."

"Now that's scary," says Jim.

When I first met Jim, he watched me practice docking in the Bayliner, only to laugh and walk away – probably he was worried about the property he so faithfully protects, and just didn't want to watch my antics any longer.

"Something nice and wide would be nice," I suggest.

"Oh," says Jim.

He looks like he's contemplating where he can put Ken's boat without a minor collision getting anyone excited.

"Have him pull in just before the *Lilian Rose*, then all the way down the next row. He can park at the end on the left side. *Fish Finder's* owner will be out of town all week, so we'll raft him up to it."

I know the *Lilian Rose*, a pink-and-turquoise monument in the South Harbour (until removed the following year). Some want it sunk as an artificial reef, which would rid the harbour of the eyesore (or historical hulk, depending on your point of view). The South Harbour is the working end of the marina, where hefty commercial fish boats are mixed with transient vessels that Jim squeezes in between.

Margy and I walk back up to the highway, where we can hike around to the fuel dock. There's no pedestrian connection between the floating fuel barge and the rest of the marina. It's a bit of a walk, but we should be well ahead of Ken.

Once we're on the barge, the rest of the chuck is blocked from view by the tall rock breakwater and the Texada Island ferry, leaving only a small opening looking out towards Malaspina Strait. The fuel dock is empty of boats. I haven't brought "lots of help," as Ken has requested. But there's no need for concern. A 28-foot boat can be easily handled by me alone as the dock crew, plus Margy is here, and the fuel attendant can assist, if necessary.

"I bet you don't get many visitors like us," I kid the young woman behind the counter, as Margy and I walk into the fuel office.

"No, most of them come by boat," answers the smiling girl. "Not many visitors by land."

"We're here to meet an brand new boat that has been in the water only a few days. From Campbell River, a 28-footer."

"Powerboat?" she asks.

I forget there's anything else. If you own a powerboat, that's all you think about. If you pilot a sailboat, it's probably quite the opposite.

"Yes, and the skipper's having a heck of a time learning to dock."

"He's come to the right place," says the always-smiling young woman who's confidently in charge today. "Lots of wide-open space here."

"He'll find something to hit," I say.

I'm kidding, of course, but it seems serendipitous that a big boat suddenly appears, coming around the corner of the rock breakwater, headed towards the fuel barge.

"It's the Coast Guard," says Margy. "They're coming here."

Sure enough, the impressive *Cape Caution*, based in the North Harbour, is headed straight in. This is a beautiful vessel, replacing the older *Mallard* in 2005. I miss seeing the *Mallard*, a ship of older design, in our local waters. But the 47-foot *Cape Caution* is a far superior ship, with a high-tech cockpit. Supposedly, this all-weather vessel can handle any seas, even able to roll completely over and right itself again. And it's coming here for fuel just when Ken is due to arrive.

Cape Caution motors in slowly, careful not to disturb the nearby docked vessels with its otherwise-substantial wake. I watch the smiling young fuel attendant standing by the pumps, but she's handling this arrival different from what I'm used to. Normally, she steps forward to the edge of the dock to lend a hand with the lines, but now she's well back from the edge, just waiting. In fact, I soon realize she's standing out of the way on purpose.

The Coast Guard vessel drifts towards the dock, facing south on the larger finger (now unavailable for Ken). The large boat kisses the rubber-faced edge of the dock, and instantaneously three crew members hop onto the fuel barge, thick docking lines in-hand. They wrap their lines around the big cleats so quickly that it looks choreographed. The big ropes swirl smoothly into place, several layers thick. No adjustment needed – Cape Caution bobs slightly, and the lines snap into perfect position.

"I guess you don't need my help," I yell to the captain, who looks down from the boat's bridge.

"No, we can handle it," he laughs.

Refueling the *Cape Caution* means a big drink. The process takes a long time, and Ken should be here any minute. I have the perfect plan, if the Coast Guard leaves before he arrives. I'll ask the captain to surprise Ken, who is undoubtedly now close to the harbour. I bet the captain could give Ken quite a welcome with the Coast Guard's bullhorn.

On the other hand, if the big boat is still here when Ken arrives, options are limited. There's no place to park except on the short dock finger, perpendicular to the Coast Guard. That means Ken will be approaching near the stern of the big vessel, and that's the expensive twin-engine end of *Cape Caution*.

As I ponder the situation, the captain goes into the office to settle up the bill. I hear the girl say: "Almost five hundred," which I assume means 500 litres rather than dollars. At today's fuel price, it's all in the same ballpark.

Here comes Ken! He rounds the rock-walled breakwater, fortunately at a reasonably slow speed. I wave and he replies with a short *toot-toot* of his horn. Most of the Coast Guard crew is on the dock now, watching the arrival of a 28-foot yellow boat, and its time to admit the situation.

"New boat – only been in the water since Friday," I announce, looking at what looks like the second-in-command. "He's struggling a bit with docking, so be ready."

They're ready. There's no way this puny yellow boat is going to hurt their expensive ship. They huddle, without any additional words from anyone, near the corner of the dock at the engine-end of *Cape Caution*. They stand ready to assist – and immediately thrust Ken away, if necessary.

It's no idle threat, because Ken points the nose of *Mr. Buttercup* directly at the corner of the dock. This would be the perfect docking entry, were it not for the Coast Guard ship extending out past the corner. And Ken keeps on coming, not at high-power, but moving awfully fast for the situation. It's impossible not to be reminded of the hero of the hilarious movie, *Captain Ron*, headed directly for a crowded dock of partying boaters.

He just keeps coming. The *Cape Caution's* captain now joins us at the corner of the dock. There's no need for him to ask questions – the situation is obvious. He stands with his troops, ready for action. They don't need any more help, so I motion for Margy to join me along the edge of the dock, where we expect (hope) Ken will arrive.

I give Ken a palm-down wave, an obvious slow-down signal. And Ken does seem to slow a bit, but his twin outboards are still in forward

gear, although probably at idle. I'd prefer he shift into neutral and just drift the rest of the way.

Ken clears the stern of the *Cape Caution* by only a few feet, so nobody has to toss Mr. Buttercup back to sea. And I'm glad he doesn't decide to kick the stern towards the dock with a shot of reverse – that would be too close.

But he never comes out of forward gear. It's going to be a pretty good bump on his bow. As Margy and I grab his front rail, I watch the Coast Guard crew – at least six hands are on *Mr. Buttercup's* stern rail, holding the boat away from the dock (and their ship!) with brute force.

I wouldn't have guessed human muscle could overcome two 150-horsepower outboards in even a minor battle, but we win. Mr. Buttercup whacks her bow against the dock with a solid thump, but the stern of the boat remains a solid metre from contacting anything. From overhead, it would have looked like a constant 5-knot arrival, followed by a sudden dead stop.

"Engines off, Ken!" I yell. We're probably pushing the huge fuel dock, *Cape Caution*, and all of us a few metres toward shore.

"Thanks!" yells Ken, as if this is a normal docking episode.

I'm waiting for something bad to happen. But without saying a word, the *Cape Caution's* captain motions for his crew to unhook their lines. They crank their engines and are gone within what seems a few seconds. No admonition, no checking of boat operator's card, no complimentary safety inspection – just a professional Coast Guard crew who probably remembered how they once had to learn boating maneuvers themselves.

I hop aboard *Mr. Buttercup* and walk through the cabin door to find Ken shutting down his electrical systems. This boat is so new I actually get a whiff of that new-boat smell.

"Made it!" says Ken. "But when I said 'Bring help,' I didn't know you'd bring the Coast Guard."

* * * * *

After refueling, I join Ken in *Mr. Buttercup* to travel the short distance to his assigned overnight docking spot. Margy has walked around to be positioned for our arrival.

Leaving the fuel dock, it's necessary to first back up a few metres and turn around. Fortunately, we're now the only boat in the area.

"I always get it backwards when I'm in reverse," admits Ken.

One thing about Ken, he's quick to admit his limitations. In reality, he's an accomplished small-boat operator who takes his responsibilities on the water seriously. But this new boat marks a new learning curve. A second thing about Ken – he learns quickly.

Okay, let's tally this up: new boat, difficulty docking, never anchored, can't back up. But dang it! – Ken's going to Alaska, and I know he'll do just fine. One thing for certain, he'll be grinning the entire way.

Under my direction, Ken turns before we reach the gaudy *Lilian Rose*, and points the bow towards Margy who marks our parking spot. Jim is there too, waiting to assist. How many wharfingers take care of their customers like this? Answer: many at small ports in British Columbia, but none of them surpass Jim.

And there's a mass of others standing on the dock too.

"Gibsonites!" I say to Ken.

"Yup." Ken smiles when he recognizes his friends from the Gibsons Yacht Club.

I'm a little uncomfortable when Ken slides a little too close to a boat on our right side he as he prepares to make the final left turn. Although it's probably unnecessary, I go out on the aft deck and push off the nearly-missed sailboat as we slip by.

The docking that follows isn't pretty, but much better than the last one. With the mass of anxious helpers, *Mr. Buttercup* is efficiently rafted up next to *Fish Finder*.

Ken and I are on the stern deck, accepting the accolades of his friends from Gibsons.

"Nice boat!" shouts one.

"Really yellow," says another.

"Is the radome supposed to hang down like that?" asks a third.

The radome isn't supposed to hang down at all. The antenna is tilted significantly, pointed at an angle toward the bow.

"Must have been some mighty rough water near Mitlenatch," I say to Ken when we inspect the antenna. "Of course, it's a new boat, and still on sea trials."

Ken and I adjust the radome. I push it back towards the level position, while Ken tightens the big nut controlling the antenna's tilt angle.

"Do you think it's important to get it perfectly level?" I say.

"Probably," says Ken, as he cranks on the nut. "But it looks pretty level now."

The Gibsonites are all in-dock now, except for Klaus and Fran who are still struggling north from Gibsons, their engine leak repaired. But plans are still changing. Some bad (worse) weather is expected to move in tomorrow. Sam, who has now arrived on the Comox ferry, joins us as we discuss the alternatives.

"Maybe we'll head back to Gibsons tomorrow, before the storm moves in," says Ken. "Sam is willing to drive the car, and I'll take *Mr. Buttercup*."

"We'll follow you in *Halcyon Days*. Heck, I still want to anchor off Molly's Reach."

This has been one of my unfulfilled goals for two years. A boat trip to Gibsons requires several days of good weather to make me feel comfortable, since it's quite a ways for the Bayliner, and there are few docks or anchorages as safe havens along the route. But we could anchor overnight in Gibsons (Molly's Reach!) and return to Powell River after the storm passes. Getting two good weather days in a row is asking a lot.

While Ken stays in the boat working on his myriad of antennas and cable connectors, I walk over to *Endless Rode*, the 34-foot sailboat from Gibsons that Gord and Marlene sailed to New Zealand. (In the first edition of *Up the Strait*, Chapter 5, I erroneously documented their Pacific Crossing as sailing to Australia in a 32-footer.) With things behind schedule because of the weather, we talk about the yacht club's revised plans. Gord, in his relaxed manner, tells me they'll spend another night here and then cruise to Grace Harbour in Okeover Inlet. If I was forced to sail across the Pacific, I'd pick Gord as my captain.

Sam, Margy, and I walk to lunch, while Ken continues setting up his electronic equipment – an Internet antenna for his laptop computer, ham radio gear, and a plethora of geeky stuff that follows him wherever he goes. Ken is the ultimate wire-head, with drawers full of adapter cords, connectors, and high-tech gizmos. I kid him that the boat is top-heavy with all of its antennas – it has six so far. Internet and ham radio connections allow Ken to talk to his boating friends from almost any port.

On our return to the dock after lunch, we walk past old wooden trawlers and hearty aluminum prawn boats that populate the South Harbour. Suddenly, Sam yells out and drops to her knees between a fish boat and a small tug.

"Oh, no! Look, that bird has fallen into the water!"

Don't birds go in the water of their own accord? Would any bird go into the water if it were not adapted to do so? Sam scoops a raven out of the water and sits it on the dock, her hands wrapped loosely around it.

"We need to warm you up," she says to the bird.

Her touch is gentle, but her hands almost surround the bird's entire body, forming a shield of human heat.

"Its just a baby," says Sam.

Even regarding this statement, I'm not so sure. This bird looks quite big, but I've probably never seen a baby raven. The bird looks dead – scraggly, wet, and unmoving. But one eye flickers slowly, showing a light blue glint that seems to pulsate. The other eye is shut tight. Barely alive, this seems hopeless. I feel for Sam as well as the bird. She holds it so purposefully. It's obvious to me, however, that she'll not succeed.

A big raven appears overhead, circling and squawking. Momma is concerned with her baby, and she's directing her anger at us. So this really is a baby, which disproves my thoughts. I hope my other conclusion – that this is incurable – is also wrong.

Momma raven lands mid-mast on a nearby sailboat, continues to squawk, but does not move closer to us. Sam holds the bird for a few more minutes, and the baby starts to squirm a bit.

"Hypothermia," says Sam. "I think it's coming back."

Back from the dead. As far as I'm concerned, it's a miracle. The bird does not struggle to get free, but it's obviously more alert. It's flickering eye is steady now, and the other eye is open a slit.

"You can go, when you're ready," Sam says, still kneeling and holding the baby. "Everything is okay."

The bird squirms a bit, and Sam loosens her grasp. She places her hands, with the baby still in them, on the dock. The raven struggles to its feet, stumbling at first and falling back to the deck. Then it stands firmly and struts away, spreading its wings and shaking them.

"It'll be okay now," says Sam. "Go find Momma!"

We walk away from the spot of the miracle, looking back over our shoulders. The bird is still standing and preening itself, looking healthier by the minute.

"Now keep out of the water, you stupid thing!" yells Sam to the alive-again bird.

This bird may be stupid, but it's infinitely lucky to have found a woman like Sam.

* * * * *

The next day's weather is as good as we can expect, but seems to be deteriorating fast. Looking northward, I watch mid-level clouds streaming toward us in advance of the next storm. The sooner we get going the better.

When Margy and I arrive at *Mr. Buttercup*, Ken and Sam are stowing gear, ready to remove the shore power cord. Sam needs to leave soon by car to catch the ferry at Saltery Bay.

"We'll get the Bayliner and bring her around to the South Harbour," I say.

"Okay, I'll be waiting for you. Where will you park?"

"I'll just raft up next to you. If you can double-park, I can triple-park. Jim won't mind."

Of course, I haven't asked the wharfinger, but it'll be a brief stay.

Margy and I leave the South Harbour to walk around to our boat, which is ready to go in the North Harbour. As Margy fills the Bayliner's water tank with the dockside hose, I warm up the engine. Within a few minutes, we're out of the breakwater, heading to the South Harbour. During this brief journey, just outside the breakwater, we encounter slapping southeast swells. The Bayliner is only 24 feet in length and less rugged than *Mr. Buttercup*. Plus, neither Margy nor I like big waves. Like flying in our Piper Arrow, when it gets bumpy, we land. Nothing is so important that we must battle relentless turbulence in the air or on the sea. There's now little doubt we're not going all the way to Gibsons today, but we can get Ken started and give the Bayliner some needed exercise.

Past the fuel dock, we continue into the harbour, turning right at the *Lilian Rose*. There are no open spots in this row, but yellow *Mr. Buttercup* is ready to receive us. We raft up easily, since I've grown accustomed to *Halcyon Days'* docking quirks. Her command bridge and slow idle makes her an easy boat to maneuver, even in close quarters like this. With his twin-engines, Ken will soon be able to outmaneuver us.

Sam grabs the bow line, and Ken handles the stern. We're successfully triple-parked – Bayliner to *Mr. Buttercup* to *Fish Finder* to dock. I no sooner step into the rear of *Mr. Buttercup* than Jim strides past on his wharfinger rounds.

"Now what?" he yells over his shoulder as he passes.

"Quick, where's my credit card?" I say to Jim. "Just your typical triple-parking maneuver, while I run into the store for a bottle of milk!"

Jim disappears down the dock, shaking his head in mock disgust.

* * * * *

I maneuver the Bayliner out of its rafted spot, backing out of the row past the *Lilian Rose*. Then I pull forward in front of the wide opening near the fuel dock, awaiting Ken.

In a few minutes, *Mr. Buttercup* rounds the corner, her yellow cabin in weird contrast to the pink and turquoise of *Lilian Rose*.

"What a colourful harbour," I say to Margy.

"In more ways than one," she replies.

"*Buttercup*, this is *Halcyon Days*. Radio check on channel sixty-nine."

"Loud and clear, *Halcyon Days*. You ready to go?"

"Ready, but don't forget the deal. You lead to break the waves for us, and don't be surprised if we break it off to head for an anchorage or back to Powell River."

"Roger, *Halcyon Days*. Let's go."

Once he's outside the breakwater, Ken throttles up, slowly at first, and we jostle into position about 50 metres behind. As Ken's wake settles down and I'm clearly on-plane, I glance at my GPS: 21.2 knots. Although Ken is already pulling away from us, this will be an ideal speed for us, conserving a bit of fuel but not holding Ken back very much."

"*Buttercup*, if you can establish 21 knots, that will be perfect for us."

"Roger, *Halcyon Days* – 21 knots."

As we approach Grief Point, a mere kilometre from the marina, it starts to get rough. At first, in Ken's wake, we don't feel it, but within another klick, swells begin to slap at us. Even the water inside the protective wake is getting lumpy.

We whack against the waves, and I see whitecaps around the point. Passing the piled-rock breakwater at Beach Gardens, I reduce power nearly to idle to more closely assess our surroundings.

"*Buttercup, Buttercup* – *Halcyon Days* is slowing down to evaluate things. It's pretty rough back here already."

"Okay. Let me know what you decide."

We watch *Mr. Buttercup* come off plane and coast nearly to a stop in front of us, waiting. The water to our left, between the Bayliner and shore, is only slightly rippled. But to our right, whitecaps extend towards Texada Island as far as we can see. I bring the throttle back to idle, just enough power to keep us pointed south.

"What do you think?" I ask Margy.

"I think it's already getting rough, and it isn't going to get any better farther south."

I nod my head. We love boating too much to make this into a miserable voyage.

"I'm sure Ken is safe in these conditions," I say.

"His boat takes the waves well," Margy replies. "We could make it too, but it wouldn't be fun."

I pick up the microphone to contact Ken. I regret another aborted attempt to anchor off Molly's Reach.

"*Buttercup*, *Halcyon Days* is turning back. We know you'll be okay, but it's already getting rough for us."

"*Buttercup* understands. I guess I'll get going then."

In front of us, Ken is already powering up, his wake starting to trail from the stern. He'll make it back to Gibsons without any trouble. But I wonder about two weeks from now, when he leaves for Alaska.

* * * * *

Ken and Sam's Alaska journey was completed safely, but with some unique incidents you might expect from Mr. Buttercup. I'm encouraging Ken to release the log of that journey (which he has already recorded) to the public, or maybe I'll tell his story my own way in a future book in this series.

◊ ◊ ◊ ◊ ◊ ◊ ◊

Chapter 5

Finding Gibsonites

Although Ken and Sam are now back home in Gibsons, getting ready for their trip to Alaska, we still want to travel north to Desolation Sound with the Gibsonites. But I'm not sure I can adapt to their sailboat speed. Although I respect the desire of others to make cruising on the chuck a slow-paced adventure, I'll probably never adjust to trawler speeds. Once you've been on-plane, it's difficult to slow down.

Thus, the revised plan – let the Gibsons Yacht Club get started first, and join them at one of their scheduled anchorages. What a great excuse to cruise – looking for Gibsonites.

On a perfect, mid-June day (after what seems like weeks of wind and rain), Margy and I depart Powell River. We plan a stop at Grace Harbour in Okeover Inlet, where we expect to find the Gibsonites.

The route north is a familiar one, although it's our first trip of the year. We motor confidently past the red Atrevida buoy, maneuvering offshore a bit to avoid a small runabout trolling along Mystery Reef. During this low-low tide, the reef is high-and-dry, an easily avoided obstacle to navigation.

I elect to cruise outside the Copeland Islands, to avoid the no-wake zone inside Thulin Passage. The water is only lightly rippled until we cross back towards Sarah Point. On the command bridge, Margy and I discuss a change in our route. We'll deviate to Refuge Cove to check on the supply of my books at the general store before the manager goes home for the day. We can refuel there, then head to Grace Harbour.

Just as we're discussing this, we cross a brief area of widely-spaced 3-foot swells. The Bayliner handles them well, settling down quickly on the other side, but there are more unexplained swells ahead. The wind does not seem to have changed, most of the water is still flat, and no large boats are nearby to create a large wake. But just north of the Copeland Islands, something has changed. Off to the left, a white-capped line of swells is flowing away from us, towards Cortes Island.

The sea is like this – unexplained changes from minute to minute that enhances your respect for its power. Maybe it's a minor tidal bore of sorts. Yet, there's no narrow inlet here, nor are we approaching a change of tide. In fact, we're close to halfway between an exceptionally low and particularly high tide in open water. That could be part of the situation – a bit of between-slack current. But I've never before seen it here, nor is this spot known for such a flow. However, as I look around, I see a variety of promontories and small islands, plus Thulin Channel behind us. It's easy to visualize a natural but undocumented confluence of water at this spot. In any case, the swells quickly pass, and we settle back into lightly rippled seas.

In another 15 minutes, we follow a 60-foot powerboat into Rufuge Cove. The yacht lowers its giant black fenders in preparation for docking, slowing to a crawl to prevent its large wake from disrupting other boats in the cove.

As we approach the fuel dock, the 60- footer veers off to the left, apparently planning to tie up at the transient dock. That gives

us plenty of room to maneuver near the gas pumps. The fuel dock is wide open, with nobody home. We expect the normal off-season instructions posted on the office door: "Pump it yourself, and take the litre reading to the store."

Just as expected, the note is on the office door. I pump 84 litres, and then Margy and I walk up to the general store to pay for the gas and coordinate sales of *Up the Strait*. The big boat we followed into the cove is already preparing to cast off, after their quick visit to the store.

"Must take more time to dock a boat like that than to buy your groceries," says Margy. "Did you see what they bought?"

"No. Not much, I'd guess, based on how quick they were in and out."

"They loaded a small bag of fruits and vegetables," replies Margy. "I bet they wouldn't have been able to find such wide-open dock space here in the summer."

It's okay for small boats (us) to make fun of big boats (them). Of course, there's some obvious jealousy involved, but we're happy boaters in our 24-foot Bayliner. A few more feet in length and a wider beam for stability in heavy seas would be nice, but there's little else we crave for cruising the chuck. To me, bigger holds little advantage and quite a few drawbacks (even before you mention cost). I love the maneuverability of the Bayliner in tight areas and during docking, and I'm content (while simultaneously challenged) to be confined to its small living space for days on end.

By the time we get back to *Halcyon Days* (the store manager has already gone home, so no books today), we're still alone on the fuel dock. We cast off quickly, and are on our way to Grace Harbour.

From here, it's a rather direct route to Malaspina Inlet, which leads into Okeover. We pass through the swirls of current near the first island at the mouth and along the islets to the right. In another 10 minutes, we enter Grace Harbour, noticing new construction along the south shore: two cabins, one particularly large. While marveling at this unexpected growth, I reflect on the historical dwindling of population in this area over the last two centuries. This was once a flourishing winter village for three Salish tribes, normally competitive, but joined together in Grace Harbour for protection against the winter storms.

Today, the anchorage is packed, at least in comparison to what we found on a previous visit, also in mid-June. Then again, eight of these boats are from the Gibsons Yacht Club (four sailboats and four powerboats). It would look almost empty without them.

The decks of all the boats are empty, as far as we can tell. Several dinghies are pulled up on shore nearby. We motor slowly past Gord and Marlene's *Endless Rode*, circle around Klaus and Fran's Uniflite powerboat anchored nearby, and then return to *Endless Rode*.

"Paging Marlene. Paging Gord," I announce, not very loudly.

I hear Marlene say something from inside their sailboat, and then she appears on deck, her typical smiling self, waving at us.

"Well, hello!" she says. "Hey, Gord, look who's here."

We really don't know each other well. There's just something about Gord and Marlene that makes you feel comfortable under any conditions, even interrupting the privacy of their anchorage.

I'm hoping for an interview for a future book (this one!) regarding the details of their gutsy Pacific crossing in *Endless Rode*. For the next few minutes, as I probe with a few questions, they discuss their amazing trip.

Gord lounges back in his usual relaxed style, while Marlene sits with an electronic bug-zapper that looks like a small, yellow tennis racket. I guess when you've sailed all the way across the Pacific, you've learned the priorities of human comfort.

* * * * *

In 1994, Gord sailed *Endless Rode* from Victoria to Hawaii with three male shipmates, sort of a combined yacht race and shakedown cruise for what was to follow. The famous annual race took 19 days. Marlene flew to Hawaii, where she joined Gord for an island-hopping voyage from there to New Zealand. From August to November, Gord and Marelene sailed westward, stopping at tropical islands along the way. After wintering in New Zealand (summer there), they began their 27-day return trip to Hawaii the following spring.

The 34-foot C & C sailboat, manufactured in Ontario, is a sturdy craft, but not so strong as to survive unscathed during fierce ocean storms. The failure of rigging tackle led to a partially-furled jib sail, entangled above the main mast's spreader (upper T-bar). During heavy winds, the stuck jib pulled on the aluminum main mast until it finally broke. Limping into port at Hawaii, *Endless Rode* remained there for six years. In 2001, Marlene and Gord brought the boat back to Canada in six weeks of non-stop sailing.

"Non-stop" is a good summary of ocean sailing in a boat like this. Maintaining your forward progress is a continual goal: "Stopping for any reason in mid-ocean makes no sense," says Gord. "You're simply too focused on getting closer to your destination."

"Day and night makes little difference," says Marlene. "At night you sleep in shifts, so it gets a bit eerie on deck."

"Of course, you're using your autopilot most of the time in the open sea," says Gord. "But the whole thing takes a lot of teamwork."

"We were always confident," adds Marlene. "Even in the worst gales, we were never afraid, because we believed in our own skills. We're self-reliant, and we felt comfortable with each other's abilities. That's important when sailing under trying conditions."

Marlene is the least experienced of the two when it comes to sailboats. She encountered bouts of sea sickness that made the trip even more demanding. When I ask her to identify her biggest concern on this trip, she quickly answers: "Weather."

"It goes back to the concept of teamwork," says Marlene. "You rely on each other in a storm, but I worried about the weather a bit. Sometimes it would blow like stink."

"Weather forecasts are worth paying attention to, but they are reliable only about three days in advance," says Gord. "In our case, we got our weather reports over HF, single-sideband, but the reports were limited. So once you're three days out of port, you just have to take whatever weather heads your way."

Gord's electronics background with Nav Canada meant no lack of radio gear for the trip, including HF communications and GPS for navigation.

"Do you use your engine when you're in stormy conditions?" I ask.

"It's the sails that give you stability," says Gord. "The engine isn't important, except during docking. In the open sea, you use the sails for control."

"What about the danger of colliding with other ships when traveling across the Pacific?" I ask. "Especially in low visibility – isn't that a concern?"

"Not really," replies Gord. "Once you're offshore and out of the shipping lanes, there's nobody there. You rely on the big Pacific High, sailing south when traveling west to take advantage of the wind, then sail to the north on the return route. The big ships go right through the center of the high – where the best weather sits – since they don't need the wind. It's pretty empty out there for small boats like us. On the stretch from Hawaii to New Zealand, we saw only one boat and talked to one other on the radio."

I ask Gord the same question I asked Marlene, regarding his biggest concern on the voyage, and his answer is the same: "Weather," he says, without pausing to ponder.

"We knew the boat inside out, so there weren't any big concerns with the equipment," says Gord. "But the weather was a continuous challenge. Still, even when we encountered waves as big as 30-feet, we were confident. You just keep sailing, wanting to get through the storm, to get it over with."

Thirty-feet – now there's a real wave!

Turning to the topic of routine sailing as they're doing this week, I ask what makes for successful teamwork aboard *Endless Rode*.

"I'm nearly always at the helm," says Marlene. "Since I'm not as experienced as Gord, I steer while he jumps all over the place, changing sails, adjusting winches. We work as a team, and it has jelled fine for us."

No doubt – they are a team. And *Endless Rode* is a beautiful boat to practice teamwork.

* * * * *

Although we could anchor with the Gibsonites in Grace Harbour, we have other plans. We bid good-bye, exit the harbour, and turn left towards Lancelot Inlet. We come up on-plane, with our sights set on (again! – we can never get enough) Theodosia Inlet.

Today, at nearly high tide, the river-like connection between Lancelot and Theodosia is easy to navigate. It's also after-hours for

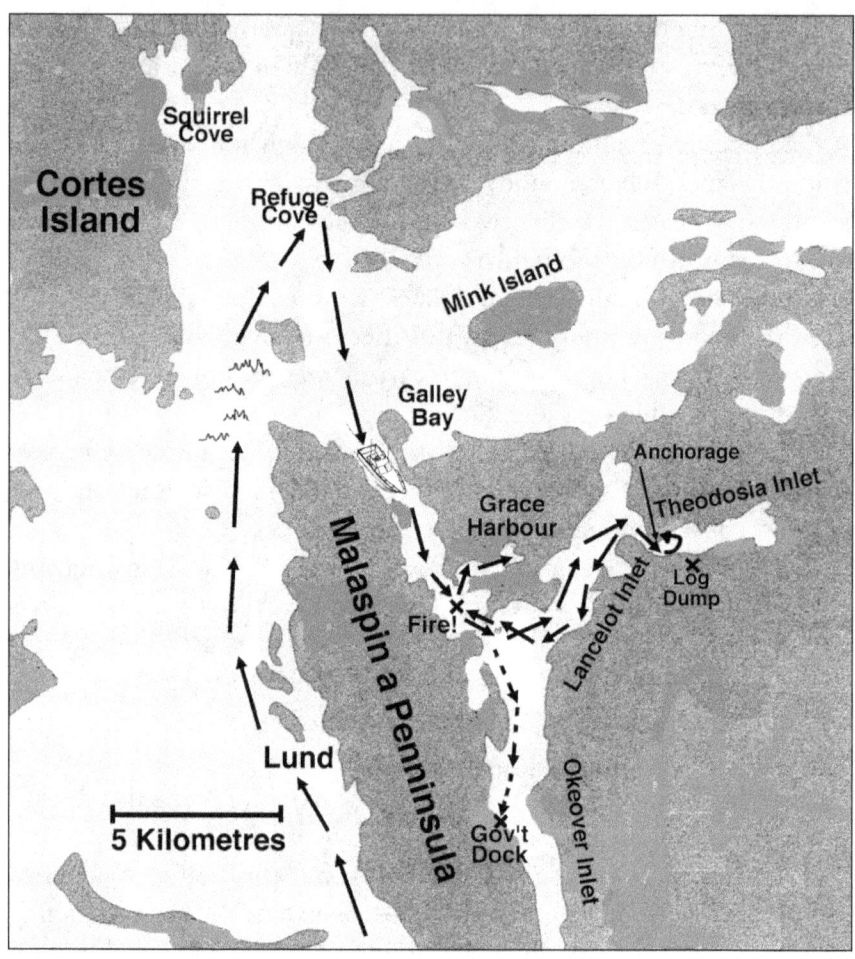

logging, so we don't expect to encounter a crew boat to give us a "Watch out!" thrill.

Entering Theo, I look right through a shallow lane of water (not navigable) to the tucked-in anchorage just inside the inlet. Around the final corner, Theodosia spreads before us, with the log booms full of timber.

We're barely within the inlet when a huge rumble nearly straight ahead identifies the drop of a bundle of logs into the water. In few seconds, we hear the delayed crash of the logs splashing into the water. Loggers working this late at night is unusual, since they normally start at dawn. I'm surprised but pleased to witness this always-exciting show.

Tucked into our favourite small cove just inside the inlet, we settle in for an early evening exhibition of logs skidding down the bank and into the chuck. According to the news media, logging operations may halt within two weeks, the result of a looming strike. Maybe management is pushing operational hours in anticipation of the shutdown.

After a flurry of vehicle activity near the log dump, a cloud of dust moves down the shoreline from the north. A log truck full of timber emerges from the cloud, coming to a stop at the dump. A skiploader pulls up to the onshore side of the truck, positioned to push the load into the water. It takes only a few minutes, and soon the bundle is sliding towards the water, seemingly in slow motion. The splashes are not as big as I've seen here before, probably because of the steep angle of the drop. And it's barely audible today because of the breeze blowing up the inlet and way from us.

A second truck arrives in another cloud of dust. This time, the logs are so long that they drag on the ground behind the truck. After watching this drop of logs into the chuck and then another, all is quiet. Then we hear the big blue (almost black) crew boat crank up and depart. It's the same boat that made so many trips into this inlet

during our visit last year. Margy and I watch it speed towards the connecting channel and out of the inlet. The sound of the engine increases as it approaches the shallow opening behind our anchorage. We watch the boat zip quickly past and out of sight. We're now alone in remote solitude.

As the evening's high tide approaches (the highest so far this month, by nearly a foot), Margy tries her hand at fishing. We've had good luck in confined areas like this near high tide.

"Will you help me get a shark off the hook, if I catch one?" she asks.

"Not here," I reply. "Way too shallow for dogfish. It's only 30-feet-deep."

"Well, I caught one last year," she reminds me.

"Really?" I ask. Then I think for a moment and remember she did catch a dogfish in this very spot.

After a few minutes, I join her, fishing from the opposite side of the boat, jigging in the shallow water. We don't catch anything, but fortunately that includes sharks.

While fishing, Margy spots a huge jellyfish, floating towards her side of the boat on the rising tide.

"It's tentacles spread about five feet," she says.
"Oh?" I reply.
"And reddish-brown too."

It's crowded on the Bayliner's aft deck with two fishing lines in the water, so I stay on my side of the boat, waiting for another jelly fish to swim by that I can see. A small one drifts by on my side of the Bayliner, but it's normal in size and a common opaque off-white. Now I regret not crowding to the other side to see the big red critter.

*****

The next morning dawns clear, with strands of cirrus clouds streaking high overhead. I'm on the aft deck early, watching the glowing colours in Theodosia's sky, a never-disappointing spectacle. The dark-blue crew boat breaks the early morning silence, swerving through the narrows, around the log boom, and into the dock.

No breakfast or even coffee this morning – we want to get through the narrows and into Lancelot Inlet before the tide gets much lower, and it's on its way down fast. Margy drives, while I set up for trolling. I'll try a Deep-Six (an amateur's alternative to a downrigger) with a flasher and a spotted Coyote Wonderbread spoon. Salmon are often caught on Coyotes around here (especially Wonderbread and Cop Car varieties), with flashers mounted in front of the lure, but it's the first time I've used this established rig. Trolling for salmon isn't my area of expertise. In fact, saltwater trolling is something I've done only a few times.

Entering Lancelot Inlet, I ask Margy to slow to idle and navigate along the shoreline, while I drop the flasher and Coyote into the water. I play out plenty of line on a flexible pole that bends so much I fear it'll break. But it's normal for salmon trolling, and the pole should be secure in its rod holder on the aft rail. Yet I don't trust it, so I wrap a bungee cord around the base of the reel and attach it to the rail. I adjust the drag on the reel so I'll be alerted to a strike.

After a while, we switch places. I climb to the command bridge, while Margy goes below to fix coffee. I navigate slowly along the edge of an underwater shelf near the shore that's clearly depicted on the GPS. Everything is going flawlessly this morning – even the finicky

depth sounder is beaming a clear picture of the ocean floor, including a few spots where the backlit display shows what looks like fish near the bottom.

We troll past several oyster farms, edging in close where the water is shallower. Of course, this is probably too shallow for salmon, so maybe I should be in deeper water. Then again, I've never heard of anyone catching a salmon in Lancelot Inlet. But, to me, it looks like fish in every respect, and salmon must pass through here on their way to Theodosia River. Of course, that's not this time of year, is it?

Trolling is an activity that's taken me a long time to adopt. It's not the technical aspects that have been most difficult to learn. Instead, it's the slow pace. This morning makes me feel I've begun to change (for the better), slowing my personal pace to enjoy trolling. Maybe someday I'll even be ready for a deep draft boat, finally coming off-plane in my journeys along the BC coastline. But I doubt it.

"You'd better get ready with your camera," I yell down to Margy. "Here comes Tom Sawyer."

Heading towards us, even close to the shore than the Bayliner, is what looks like a giant raft. As the boat comes closer, it veers towards

a nearby oyster farm, and now I recognize a skookum landing craft rather than a flimsy raft. This is an oyster farmer tending his lease, and his boat is impressively sturdy and massive.

We troll all the way to the entrance of Lancelot Inlet, finally crossing to the north shore. We're in much deeper water now, and still there are no strikes. But the coffee tastes great, the sweet-rolls are delicious, and the low morning sun is warm. I take off my jacket and strip off my long-sleeve shirt. It's already time for T-shirt and shorts.

Margy is driving now, and I ask her to head towards the rock near the point. This hazard to navigation (but safe, if closely watched) rises above the water at low tide. Already it's out of the water and full of life. A cluster of birds and a dozen seals bask in the sun.

"Get in real close, right near the rock," I say to Margy. "The dropoff is steep, so there's no problem with the prop. But the fishing line might get hung up, so be ready to come out of gear if the lure catches on something."

This looks like the ideal spot for fish, so I add a second line to the water. This time, I cast and retrieve a fish-like plug, a combination of jigging and trolling. Margy navigates close to the rock, but seemingly far enough away to assure our own safety. A few seals slip off the rock, bobbing in the water nearby, inspecting us closely. I look down and see bottom.

"Hard right!" I holler, and Margy reacts immediately.

Then I realize it's not bottom that I see. Instead it's seaweed, thick flat leaves of dark green.

"It's seaweed," I say. "Shift into neutral, and I'll reel in."

Just as I speak, the trolling line zings. The drag on the reel spins as it should when encountering an obstacle (or a fish). Margy is in neutral now, and I quickly reel in my casting line before it snags, and then turn to the trolling rig. My efforts are thwarted a bit by the bungee cord on the reel, but I'm soon retrieving my line.

It's a stiff resistance on the other end, but a Deep-Six plus flasher is probably to blame, rather than a fish. I could be dragging some seaweed too. Nothing seems to be tugging on the pole, but I've been fooled before.

With a lot of line out, it takes quite a while to reel in, especially with the stiff resistance. The lure is clean, with not even a hint of seaweed.

All of this occurs with the engine in idle. Simultaneously, as I wind in my line, Margy and I watch the Gibsonites exiting Grace Harbour. What timing!

It's an impressive procession of boats, all motoring slow, the powerboats keeping pace with the sailboats. The air is calm, so sails are down. The sailboats' small engines set the speed of the parade. The last two boats out are *Endless Rode* and the powerboat *Sea Slipper*.

With both fishing poles finally secure, I return to the command bridge and take the helm. I add power, enough to accelerate and join the Gibsonites, but not so much as to create a large wake. The boats from Gibsons are less than a kilometre in front of us, and we'll catch up quickly. *Sea Slipper*, the 31-foot Uniflite, is just now making its turn into mid-channel, with *Endless Rode* in front by only a few hundred metres.

As the engine power comes up, an unusual sound emanates from the stern; unusual but not frightening. To me, it sounds like an airflow noise, maybe something flopping in the breeze near the swim-grid. I

look back, see nothing unusual, and then look at Margy sitting beside me on the command bridge.

"A gurgling sound," she says.

She hears water; I hear air.

Now we're pulling up behind *Sea Slipper*, so I maneuver to the right to pass. Both Fran and Klaus wave from their command bridge. We wave back. Then Fran waves again, differently this time, pointing to our stern with a sense of alarm.

The engine sounds normal now – the unusual noise gone – but our power is low. It's not easy to compare our performance to normal when we're off-plane like this. The Bayliner's RPM gauge has been inoperative for over a year, with no real priority to get it fix. I set cruise power by the position of the throttle and the sound of the engine, and I really don't miss the tachometer.

Suddenly a crackling noise, maybe best described as loud popping, seems to erupt from the engine compartment, below and behind us. I cut the throttle, more suddenly than I'd normally do. Glancing over my shoulder, I see smoke pouring out of the edges of the engine cover.

Nearly simultaneously, I hear Margy yell: "Smells hot!"

The engine idles with a normal sound, but I immediately turn off the ignition. As I drift to a stop, *Sea Slipper* passes the Bayliner and then quickly reverses course and comes back. Klaus brings his powerboat to a stop 10 metres away, bow-to-bow with our boat. He turns *Sea Slipper's* helm over to Fran and quickly climbs down from the command bridge to the forward deck, ready to throw us a line if we need it.

"I'm going for the fire extinguisher and a bucket!" I yell, climbing down the ladder from the command bridge.

My eyes are on the engine compartment hatch. White smoke is pouring out in increasing ferocity, along all edges of the hatch, so I step well clear as I swing my body into the cabin. The fire extinguisher is over the door, right above the sill on the inside, and it comes off its bracket with a single sweep of my fingers over the metal hinge.

Inside the cabin, I open the door to the head to grab a bucket, but it isn't there. Glancing back at the rear deck, the entire area is still smoking, but it seems somewhat less billowing.

"Where's the bucket?" I holler.

"Under the table!" Margy yells back immediately.

I grab the handle of the bucket and transfer the small fire extinguisher to the same hand. With my other hand, I reach out the door, near the engine compartment lid. I don't feel any heat, so I tap the compartment with one finger, and it's cool. For a brief moment, I consider opening the compartment, but I figure this could make things substantially worse. Right now the smoke is dissipating quickly, so if there is a fire, it seems to be dying out. Feeding the flames with a sudden influx of air seems suicidal, and I visualize flames leaping out at me. So I carefully step onto the engine lid, lean over the starboard side, and dip the bucket into the water, filling it nearly full. Then I quickly climb back up the ladder to the command bridge, where Margy waits.

"Take these, I say," handing her the fire extinguisher and the bucket.

Sea Slipper is standing by in case we need to abandon ship, and that's a comforting feeling, but all seems to be settling down now. The smoke has nearly stopped, and *Endless Rode* is already swinging into position next to us, having turned around when Klaus reported our problem on the radio.

"I'm going to wait a few more minutes before I open the engine compartment," I holler to Klaus and Fran.

"Sounds good," yells Klaus. "We've notified the Coast Guard, and they're standing by if you need them. For now, they only request we keep them informed."

"Thanks!"

Enough time seems to have elapsed now, the smoke is nearly gone, and I'm concerned with evaluating the engine situation so I can tell the Coast Guard whether we need assistance. Klaus should be able to tow me to the Okeover government dock, or I can use my dinghy's kicker, installing it on the swim-grid mount.

I climb back down the ladder, and cautiously crack open the engine lid. A little residue of white smoke pours out, but it clears quickly. All looks normal inside: no evidence of fire or even a feeling of excess heat, no significant bilge water, no oil sprayed anywhere. I reach over the engine to check the oil dipstick. It reads *Full*, and I repeat the oil check after wiping the stick clean with a rag – still *Full*.

I return to the command bridge, leaving the engine compartment open. Gord is now in his dinghy, rowing towards us from *Endless Rode*, prepared to paddle closer to assist.

"Oil level is fine," I report to Gord and the others. "I'm going to check the engine water level in a few minutes, but I want to let it cool first."

This stern-drive engine has a heat exchanger that uses inflowing cold ocean water along with self-contained fresh water. The fresh water is accessed by a pressurized cap that should not be opened when the engine is hot. I have no intention of trying to restart this engine until my friend, John, can look everything over, even though it will mean towing or motoring with the kicker several kilometres to the government dock and leaving the boat there. As soon as possible, I want to provide the Coast Guard with assurance that our situation is stable.

A long metal open boat, blunt nosed at both ends and powered by a big outboard, pulls close to lend assistance. I wave the three fishermen away with a shout: "Thanks! – everything's okay now."

After waiting a while longer, I carefully crack the pressurized cap, and steam pours out and quickly disappears. Then I open the cap farther (more steam), wait for the opening to clear, and finally look inside. Dry as a bone.

I hear the Coast Guard now, broadcasting to Klaus: "*Sea Slipper*, change to channel eight-three-alpha," says the voice.

They are switching the conversation from the general emergency frequency, channel sixteen, and moving it to a private channel. My radio has been off, so I hustle to the command bridge and switch it on.

"Can you help me find channel eighty-three alpha?" I say to Margy.

The radio on the command bridge is below the instrument panel, with a digital frequency display that's difficult to see, especially in the sun. Margy has better eyes than I do, and she's used to tuning the radio to alpha frequencies.

"You're on eighty-three 'A' now," she says.

I turn up the volume, adjust the squelch until it barely breaks, and transmit almost immediately. Klaus has contact with the Coast Guard, but I want to apprise them of my situation directly.

"Comox Coast Guard, this is powerboat *Halcyon Days* on channel eighty-three-alpha."

"*Halcyon Days*, this is Comox. You're loud and clear. Go ahead."

"*Halcyon Days* is now stable, and there's no further smoke from our engine, nor is there a fire," I report in my best airline pilot voice. "We are safe and have assistance at our location from *Sea Slipper* and *Endless Rode*, who will help us get back to a nearby dock."

"Roger, *Halcyon Days*. Please remain on this frequency for now, and report your status once you're under tow."

Gord is already hooking up a towing bridle to the rear of Sea Slipper, and when he's finished, he brings the tow rope to me.

"Can you get on the bow to tie the rope?" asks Gord.

"Sure!"

I climb along the port-side catwalk to the bow, where Gord hands me the rope.

"You can hook it to that bow cleat," says Gord. "Klaus doesn't feel real comfortable towing you, but he's willing to give it a try."

"I understand. We can hook up our kicker, if we need to. But it's not very powerful, only 3 horsepower."

"That'll take forever to get you to the Okeover dock," says Gord. "Klaus is okay with it, now that we've got things hooked up. Oh, here comes the Coast Guard!"

Bearing down on us at high speed is a bright orange, twin-engine inflatable boat. I didn't expect the Coast Guard to respond with a rescue craft, but here they are.

Gord paddles away to meet the orange inflatable, which comes to a halt about 10 metres off the Bayliner's stern. The three Coast Guard crew members are all standing, and one already has pulled out a small spiral pad, either taking notes or running a checklist.

"All is stable now!" I yell to the rescue boat. "But I don't want to risk restarting the engine."

Gord talks to the Coast Guard crew for a few minutes, and then the inflatable motors closer, pulling up beside us. Still on the command bridge, Margy and I converse with them about our situation. A call comes in on the radio, and the boat's captain takes a moment to answer it, while the note-taking crew member asks us for some basic data about our boat. The female crew member maintains her position at the helm.

"Would you like us to give you a tow?" says the boat's young captain, when he's done with his radio call.

The even younger female crew member stands at the helm, her right hand on the twin throttles. The notebook carrying fellow stands at the stern, still writing.

"*Sea Slipper* is willing to tow us to the Okeover government dock," I say. "But I don't think he feels real comfortable about it. So if you're willing to give us a tow, that would be great!"

Their vessel, a Hurricane 733 Zodiac, is 7.3 metres long, powered by twin Evenrude 150's. It's a fine colour combination – orange and black boat, white outboards, and orange rescue suits. This boat means business, and the crew is friendly and ready for any task. They cruised over from their summer station at Cortes Bay when they heard the initial call from Klaus to the Comox Coast Guard.

"We make medical evacuations at the Okeover dock, so it'll be good for these two to see the dock configuration," says the boat's captain. "They're summer interns."

"Hey, that's a great job for students," I say. "She even gets to drive."

The sunglass-clad young woman has stood at attention at the helm until now, looking serious and making fine adjustments to the throttle and wheel to keep her boat precisely parallel to the Bayliner. Now she cracks a smile.

"They do everything," says the boat's captain. "I just help them out if they need it. So now we'll hook up the towing rope. You don't need to do a thing."

"Cool!" I say, and I mean it.

The captain laughs and begins instructing his interns regarding rigging the tow line.

Gord unhooks the line from *Sea Slipper*, and paddles away in his dinghy as the Coast Guard takes charge of the tow. I wave to Gord

with heartfelt thanks. In a few minutes, the inflatable is out front, the rope slack but ready to tow.

The captain checks in with Comox on the radio, letting them know they are beginning the tow: "Comox, this is Coast Guard five-zero-nine, commencing tow of *Halcyon Days*."

"Roger, that is approved. Tow is authorized to nearest safe port."

The inflatable pulls forward to take up the slack in the tow line, as the captain calls us on the radio.

"Halcyon Days, can you switch over to channel six-one alpha now?" he asks over the radio.

"Switching to channel six-one-alpha," I reply.

"Okay, you're there," says Margy, as she clicks the radio to the new frequency.

"*Halcyon Days* is checking in on channel six-one-alpha," I report.

"Roger, *Halcyon Days*, you're loud and clear. Just sit back, and we'll tow you to the dock. Give us a call if you have any problems."

"Ready to tow," I respond.

I'm in my element now. My military background, coupled with four decades of talking to air traffic control, make me feel right at home with this team.

I wouldn't have done this on purpose for a chapter in one of my books, but I've been accused of lesser crimes. As we start moving forward, I pull out my author's notebook and start taking notes. Of course, my camera has already been plenty busy.

At first, the tow is slow. Then the ride quickens, and I notice the Coast Guard captain looking back, with his thumb held high. I counter with a quick raised thumb, indicating the faster pace is fine.

Once all settles down, Margy and I begin to think about the logistics. We can call John for a ride, but a taxi will work if he isn't home. Margy calls John on her cell phone, and Helen answers. John is up the lake, and Ed has hurt his back and shouldn't drive today. That's not a problem, but we'd prefer to ask the taxi company for one of John's brothers, Rick or Rob.

"Rick's out back, with his taxi in the air, on jacks, probably working on the brakes," says Helen. "And Rob is over on the island today," meaning Vancouver Island.

When Margy is finished, I ask to talk to Helen before she hangs up. Margy hands me the phone.

"I told you we'd close our float plan when we got home," I tell Helen. "I just didn't know it would be when we're being towed by the Coast Guard."

I often notify Helen when we're departing and returning from the chuck, a bit of free insurance and certain search and rescue, if we don't return on schedule. Helen gets a good laugh out of today's float plan closure.

After hanging up, we still have lots of time to kill. The Okeover dock is a long ways at this speed. So I telephone David, our house-sitter in California. Today is his university graduation ceremony. Although we can't be with him today, we can wish him well in the middle of our unusual day. When he answers, he explains that we've caught him at a unique time.

"Guess where I am right now?" he says.

"Don't know. Where?" I ask.

"I'm at the stadium," he says. "In the middle of graduation rehearsal."

"Can you talk now?" I ask.

"Sure. Nothing's happening. Just a bunch of people standing around in 90-degree [Fahrenheit] heat, listening to a blaring loudspeaker. Hope it's more exciting tonight."

"I'm sure it will be. We wish we could be there." (I lie.) "And Margy and I wanted to let you know how proud we are of your university degree." (The truth.) "It's a great accomplishment."

"Thanks," he replies.

I can picture David's surroundings. I've been in this urban California stadium many times, including in the heat of June. It's quite a contrast to coastal BC.

"Now guess where we are," I say.

"At your float cabin," he replies.

"No. Margy and I are sitting on the command bridge of our Bayliner, with a long yellow rope in front of us, hooked to an orange Coast Guard boat, being towed back to the dock. Our engine blew up."

"No way!" says David. "That's certainly the most unusual graduation phone call I'll get today."

"Gotta' go," I say. "The Coast Guard is calling."

And I'm serious about it, because the inflatable is calling us on the radio now, so I quickly hang up the phone.

"*Halcyon Days*, we're going to slow down and prepare for docking. We'll shorten the line first. Is it okay to dock on your port side?"

I hand the phone to Margy, and pick up the microphone. I really don't recognize "port" and "starboard" as I should, but either side is okay with mw.

"That'll be fine," I reply.

Then I think through things, identifying the left side of the boat as the port side. It's our preferred side for docking. We've stopped now, and the crew is shortening the tow line, bringing their boat back to our right (starboard) side. Oh, I see now – they'll tie their boat to our starboard side and then motor into the dock with our boat tied to them, putting our left side at the dock.

They tie up to our right side. The two interns do the work, while the captain offers a few suggestions. Students like these, I remind

myself, are a direct reflection on the excellence of the teacher. I'm certain the Coast Guard is among the best in the world when it comes to professional instruction.

Once we're secured to their boat, the female helmsman works the throttles and wheel in this critical part of the docking maneuver. This isn't a large dock, and there's limited space to bring us against the railing. The woman's instructor stands at her side, both facing forward, but she's the one moving the throttles and turning the wheel. He stands next to her, hands in his pockets, but I know he's ready to intervene if it's necessary. It reminds me of a good flight instructor, hands in his lap and feet flat on the floor during landing, providing the student pilot with needed confidence. But if the student drops a wing, the instructor is ready to take the yoke and get his feet on the rudders immediately. Building confidence while practicing vigilance is an important part of one-on-one training.

"Should I assist with the lines when we reach the dock?" I ask, now being able to talk to the boat's captain by merely speaking down to him from the command bridge. "Or should I just stay out of the way."

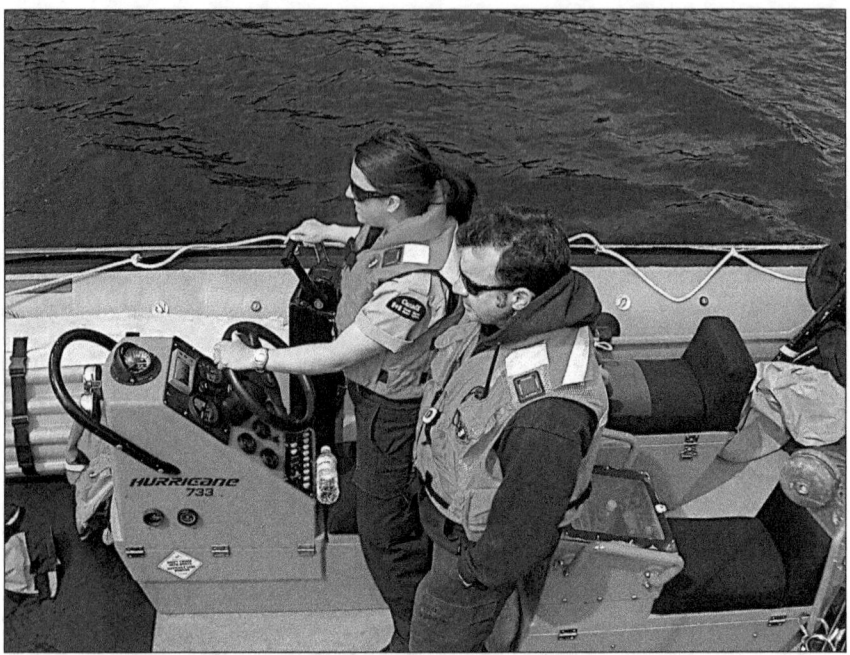

He laughs, but answers truthfully: "It might be best if you just relax and let us take care of it."

So we do, and it's a joy to watch. The Bayliner comes into port at Okeover slowly and precisely, barely kissing the dock. When I climb down the stairs from the command bridge, the crew is already tying our lines. I look over the aft rail at the boat's captain and say: "Permission to come ashore."

He laughs and pops me a sharp salute: "Permission granted."

We spend a few more minutes providing the student with the notebook the required information he needs regarding our boat and engine.

"Can I use your name as the boat's owner?" the young man asks Margy. He seems tentative about this, probably wondering whether she'll claim the position.

"Sure," she replies cheerfully.

Then she spells her complete name, adding a Canadian "zed" at the end of "Lutz" to prove we're really Canadians.

* * * * *

Afterwards:

John and I return to Okeover two days later to troubleshoot the engine malfunction. We find a blown rubber duct behind the starboard header, where hot exhaust exits the engine after being cooled by ocean water. We clean the header's water-shrouded passages with a coat hanger and replace the duct. The port side is similarly affected, with evidence of overheat and a overly-soft rubber duct, so we clean that header and replace its duct too. We fill up the reservoir, and start the engine. It runs flawlessly.

We hypothesize that the Bayliner pulled some seaweed through the raw water intake tube when we stopped to haul in my fishing line near the semi-submerged rocks. The intake tube is located on the stern leg, thus blocking off the cool ocean water's access to the heat exchanger. The result was an overheated engine when we tried to catch up with the Gibsonites leaving Grace Harbour, probably compounded by years of inattention to the headers. What poured out of the engine compartment was steam (not smoke) from a neglected and then clogged cooling system.

I regret not attending to the cooling system earlier, and I should have watched the temperature gauge more closely, since it probably would have provided a warning. But I learned a lot in the process. And I was privileged to meet the Coast Guard, up close and personal.

Center-of-Book Photos

Westview Harbour, looking south (before 2011 renovation)

Mr. Buttercup in Cortes Bay

Westview Harbour Wharfinger, Jim Parsons (right), with Author

HMCS Edmonton, coastal defense vessel, Westview Harbour

Mitlenatch Island, looking west towards Vancouver Island

Halcyon Days headed up Powell Lake

Copeland Islands and Thulin Passage, looking south
(Piper Arrow fuel consumption checklist reflected in window)

Okeover Inlet, looking south

Chapter 6

Solo Voyage

One of my greatest joys in Canada is doing things alone. Although I always enjoy the company of Margy, John, and (sometimes) others, I'm a loner. At least I recognize that fact and accept it. Where better to enjoy being a loner than in the sublime majesty of the British Columbia coast? And where easier to find opportunities to be alone than in the wilderness or on the water, or both?

I've made numerous solo voyages on the chuck, including overnight adventures as far north (so far) as the Octopus Islands and the other Hole in the Wall, where notorious currents form whirlpools and strong eddies remain even at slack tide. Some of my greatest memories in the Bayliner are in remote anchorages by myself, sometimes in challenging winds, depending solely upon my own skills. Swinging on the hook, solo style, with little wind and sunny skies is particularly inspiring.

I'm comfortable alone in the Bayliner for days on end, without any need to escape from the boat in the dinghy, *Mr. Bathtub*. It's a time to read, write, catnap in the V-berth under an open hatch, listen to the radio, soak up the sun, and just enjoy a sense of self-sufficiency.

When the opportunity for a few days alone on the chuck presents itself, I'm ready to respond. In this case, July's weather is playing games. At the airport, I watch Margy climb aboard a Pacific Coastal Beech 1900C under gray skies, with a forecast that indicates several days of rain. Each day the probability of precipitation (POP) is scheduled to rise. Two days from now, the POP forecast is 90 percent, normally an indicator of strong winds along with the rain. As I drive back from the airport, I change my plans – I'll spend the next three days solo at my floating cabin rather than on the chuck. It's an alternative that's far from frustrating. If the chuck rates a "10" on the solo scale, my cabin is at least a solid "9."

I have several chores in town, and it's after 1 o'clock before I enter the grocery store. Since the food at the cabin is in pretty good shape, I only need to replenish a few things: milk, eggs, corn on the cob, ground beef, and chicken. I select large packets of meat, since the freezer at the cabin is not packed over-full as it often is.

When I push my buggy out of the store, I'm hit by warm air and a nearly cloudless sky. The forecast for increasing cloudiness has missed the mark, and I immediately think of the ocean. On the drive back to the condo, I inspect the chuck as I come down the hill. The water is nearly flat, with pockets that are perfectly smooth

It's not too late to change my mind. But it's too late to buy the right things for a two-night boat trip. Not too late relative to time, but too late relative to my limited grocery store patience. So I take the groceries intended for the cabin to the condo, freezing the chicken and ground beef. The eggs and corn go into the refrigerator. I pour out some of the milk into a smaller container and put it in an ice pack, adding what seems appropriate from the refrigerator – soda, leftover pizza, and a half-eaten apple pie. I remove a few snacks from the cupboards, and I'm ready to go.

As I load the boat at the North Harbour, Carol yells from the adjacent dock: "Hey, Wayne, you're everywhere today!"

"It's not me who's everywhere, Carol!" I yell back.

Carol and Bruce are avid outdoors people, particularly involved in boating and quadding. Now they're unloading their boat after a few hours fishing. I always seem to run into Carol wherever I go. Already today, I've seen her at Canadian Tire, then at the bank. She's everywhere.

I pack the Bayliner quickly and am ready to go. I start the engine and unhook the lines, taking a last scan around me as I wait for the motor to warm up enough to slip smoothly into gear. The tide is ebbing, which means I'll be anchoring near high tide. That increases my options, although I haven't yet decided where I'm going. I plan to start north, stop for fuel at Lund, and probably continue to Desolation Sound for the first night. However, that route includes crowded July anchorages, unless I select spots off the beaten track.

I maneuver out of the North Harbour with only a general plan in mind. Often, that makes a cruise on the chuck even more enjoyable.

*****

At Lund, the fuel dock is nearly full. One side of the parking area is gobbled up by a large yacht of old, classic design. At first, I think I can sneak in on the other side, between a large Zodiac and a small runabout. While maneuvering close to shore to set up my approach, I stall the engine. As I drift closer to land, I'm frantic to get the engine going again, and I nearly kill the battery under the heavy load of the starter. But then the engine catches – *vroom, vroom* – all is well again.

I decide it's too tight between the two boats. So I maneuver to the outer end of the dock, where I'm afraid the gas hose won't reach. But I dock easily, and I'm close enough to the pump. The young fuel attendant hands me the nozzle.

"Gas?" he asks, in confirmation of my engine type.

"Yup," I reply. "Looks like a busy day."

"We pumped more fuel today than any day yet this summer," he replies. "Even though it's a weekday."

"I passed several trawlers coming up from Powell River," I say. "They should be here soon. Of course, hard to say if they're stopping for fuel."

I'm paying more attention to talking than refueling. While we talk, the nozzle kicks off, and I think I see a small spurt out the vent. This tank must be babied to get it full. If you don't slow down for the last few gallons, it tends to spurt out the vent prematurely, even though the tank isn't full. So I start pumping again, slower now, but I see another spurt from the vent. So I stop again and hand the nozzle back to the attendant.

While the young man goes back to the fuel shed to compute my bill, I tidy up the cabin for a quick departure. Already, a large sailboat is hovering off the dock, waiting for me to leave. Since the runabout next to me has just left, the sailboat should fit on the end spot just fine.

"Thirty-four litres," says the fuel attendant, when I get to the shack.

"Are you sure?" I ask. "It should've been more."

"I can charge you for more, if you like."

I laugh and pay my bill, but I should've taken at least 60 litres. If I'd paid more attention to the fueling process and pumped slower, the vent spurt would've been avoided, and I'd have a topped-off tank. But I have lots of fuel, including a full auxiliary tank. Meanwhile, the sailboat is still waiting for my spot. Otherwise, maybe I'd have considered pumping some more gas.

I start my engine, unfasten my lines, and efficiently exit the dock. Once I'm a few hundred metres offshore, I turn off the engine and let the boat drift. I climb down from the command bridge, dig my cell phone out of my backpack, and make three phone calls that'll take care of all the necessary business for the next few days. It's nice to get these commitments out of the way, marking the real beginning of my solo voyage.

* * * * *

I navigate up Thulin Passage, past three boats anchored in the Copeland Islands' main bay. When I'm past this no-wake zone, I creep up behind a large sailboat going the same way, move over to the right, and throttle up to pass. Once clear of the sailboat, I continue up onto plane and point the Bayliner's nose at Sarah Point. By now, I've formulated a plan for tonight – I'll continue all the way up Desolation Sound's Homfray Channel, anchoring in either Forbes Bay or in Atwood Bay near Toba Inlet. I've never been this far up Homfray, but the northern anchorages should be less crowded than popular spots to the south. Although they aren't documented in my cruising guides, I'm getting accustomed to judging anchoring conditions based on charted depth contours and visible topography. It'll be fun to try anchoring where the experts haven't drawn recommended anchoring spots on cove diagrams.

I pass between Mink Island on my right and West Redondo Island. A sailboat directly headed is on my same path, so I swing to the left to pass at a comfortable distance.

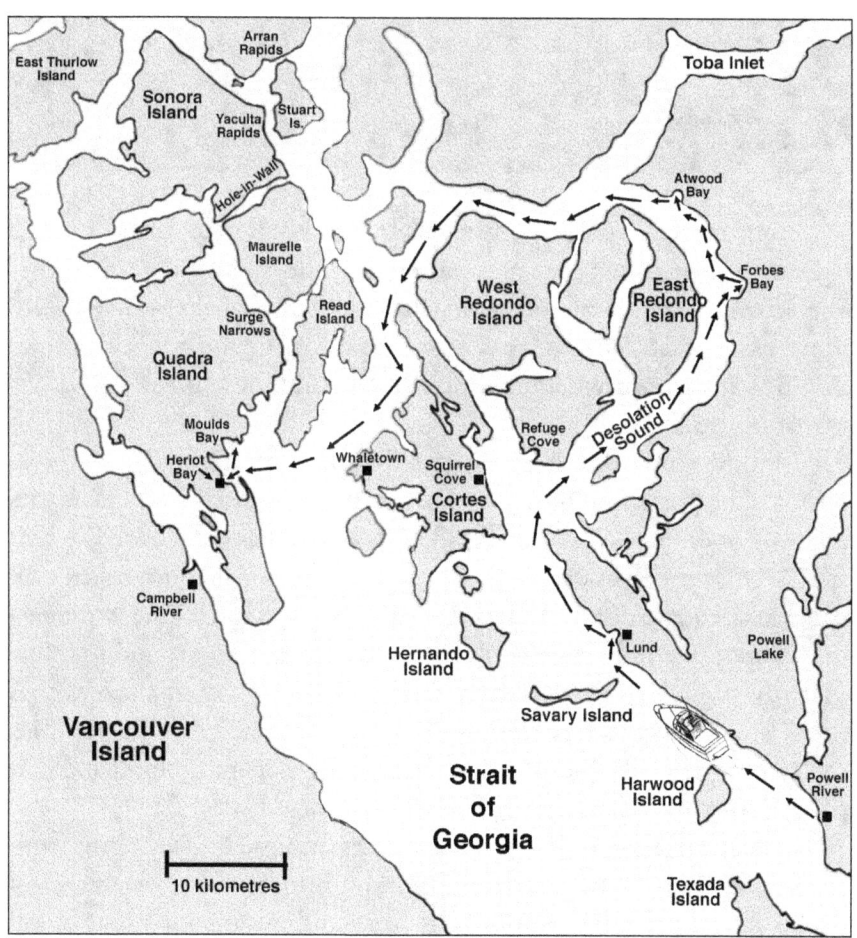

Homfray Channel is dominated by East Redondo Island on one side and the glaciated coastal mountains of the mainland on the other. The setting reminds me of Goat Island in Powell Lake, but East Redondo is a steep, angled peak in comparison to the rounder slopes of Goat. It's an overwhelming taste of the sublime – unspoiled peaks thrust up from the sea.

I follow along the shore of East Redondo for a while, then cross over to the mainland side. As Forbes Bay approaches, I check the contour lines on the GPS to decide where I'd like to anchor. The best spot seems to be just around the point, where a shallow beach will provide adequate depth. But as soon as make the turn, I see two boats in this spot, the only vessels in the bay. It makes me feel good to know that my pre-selection was what they chose, but I wish they weren't there, since two boats is plenty for this space. The other possibilities for anchoring look questionable, but I'll give them a closer look. If they don't work, I'll continue farther north to Atwood Bay.

I select a likely spot in a shoreline recess around a rocky point from the two anchored boats. I drop my hook into 50 feet of water, a bit deeper than I prefer. A shelf is likely here, and my anchor seems to fall off it, not holding properly. I retract the rode part way, move a bit, and try lowering it again. After two more tries, I fully pull up the anchor and prepare to move on. When the chain comes aboard (connecting the rode to the anchor), I find a broad knot in the chain. It's the first time I've seen such a twist in the metal chain, and I can visualize how it may have detracted from the anchor's holding ability. I unravel the chain, but decide not to try again at this spot. I move towards the river inlet, where a broad beach offers shallower water.

Near the shore, I drop anchor in 30 feet of water, but the bottom is sand or gravel, and the hook drags. I try a bit farther up the beach, but as I back the Bayliner to verify the hook is set (it isn't), I notice a blue tent in the trees. Even if the anchor grabs properly, it won't be comfortable this close to campers. So I retract the anchor again, and head for Atwood Bay.

By now it's after 8 o'clock, but there's still plenty of summer sunlight. I'd like to get established for the night soon, and I definitely don't want to be looking for an anchorage after dark. With the steep-sloped shoreline, there aren't a lot of possibilities in this area.

I visualize the outline of the next two bays, unnamed on my chart. Both are good possibilities for anchoring, although Atwood Bay is only a few kilometres ahead.

Rounding the point at the first bay, I'm surprised to see a new resort under construction. It's nearly finished, but there's no sign of workers this evening. A partially finished dock and two mooring balls float nearby. I wouldn't feel comfortable using one of the new resort's mooring floats, but the water near the dock looks promising for anchoring. The fresh construction seems to contradict my desire to be alone, but there are no people visible. Besides, I'm not sure how many boats I'll find at Atwood Bay. So I ease in towards the dock to drop my anchor.

Suddenly, appearing from nowhere, a woman walks along the shore. She's headed towards a red quad, which I now see for the first time. So this spot isn't without people. I'm outta' here.

The next bay is full of fish farm docks and a major onshore set of buildings. So I continue northward and enter Atwood Bay. Two boats are already anchored here. One is near the entrance, and the other is in the back of the bay.

I try anchoring near the log dump ramp in the back of the bay, as far from the other boat as I can. I have trouble getting the hook to hold again, but finally I give in to letting the Bayliner swing on the anchor's weight alone. With calm conditions and a protected cove, it should be safe. But this isn't the way anchoring is supposed to be handled. Sometimes, you just have to give in, and after a long day of aborted attempts, I'm ready to do just that.

It isn't exactly the privacy I'd hoped for, with another boat nearby. But it's a beautiful spot, a pleasant evening, and mountains surround me. Cloud cover now casts a somewhat sinister shadow over Desolation Sound. The Bayliner floats near the log ramp, with sharp-faced East Redondo Island projecting high to the southwest.

I go to bed battling no-see-ums that are attracted to my book light. So I stop reading, turn off the light, and comfortably drop off to sleep in the V-berth.

* * * * *

The next morning dawns drizzly, but with calm winds. On the water, I'll take calm over clear any day. While downing a breakfast of apple

pie and milk, I look over my charts, boating guides, and tide tables. The first two potential routes I look at don't fit with the tides. In fact, when pushing north in this area, with tides flooding to the south, it's tough to make more than one set of rapids at a time. So Big Bay on Stuart Island (which may not have fuel anyway) isn't going to work. It lies between two rapids, and I won't have time to refuel and make both of them on the same slack tide.

I consider Beazley Passage (in Surge Narrows), but I'll need fuel first, so I won't make it in time for the next slack tide. I finally give in to getting gas leisurely at Heriot Bay, then heading north to anchor on eastern Quadra Island. The Heriot Bay Inn is also a good lunch stop, and the gift shop may want to buy my books. So I leave Atwood Bay with a revised plan – an unhurried ride out of Desolation Sound with no time constraints to contend with.

The weather looks rather threatening, and I haven't been able to receive the marine weather report on VHF since yesterday afternoon. As Homfray Channel merges with Toba Inlet, the marine report comes in partially garbled over a background of static. But by listening to the recording several times, I determine that the forecast is nearly perfect for the next two days. The ocean buoy report at Sentry Shoal is finally back in service again, after a month of inactivity. It's a reporting station I've missed, since it's the closest off-shore marine reporting location relative to Powell River. Today it reports all of the details, including nearly calm sea conditions and a rising barometer.

The marine weather synopsis indicates a low pressure system is moving into Oregon, bringing stormy weather to that area. Rain showers may hang around here for a while, but the major action is to the south. Best of all, strong winds are not in the picture for the Strait of Georgia or the area immediately north.

The gray-black skies give Desolation Sound a gloomy and forbidding appearance, with the tall mountains providing a feeling of isolation, probably much like those days when Captain Vancouver first named this region. The sudden roiled green hue of the glacial water where Homfray Channel meets Toba Inlet adds to the sensation.

On the command bridge, there's a chill in the air, so I pull on a long-sleeve shirt. I exit Desolation Sound with a reminder to myself of

the meaning of the word "immense." Coupled with the small size of my boat, the feeling is humbling.

To the west and north, the sky is brighter, and that fits well with my planned route. As I cross over to Sutil Channel on the north side of Cortes Island, the sea surface smoothes even more, and I settle in for a nice ride to Heriot Bay.

Lots of flotsam rests in lines, but it's scattered, so I weave around it without slowing. Numerous kayaks are out today, and I give them a wide berth.

As I approach Heriot Bay, the ferry from Cortes to Quadra Island beats me in. It turns in a sweeping arc, in a stern-to-shore docking maneuver. I cut power and shift into neutral, waiting for the ferry to pull into its berth.

When all settles down, I pull in at the fuel dock near the ferry. A blond, bushy-haired teenage boy in shorts and T-shirt greets me.

"No gas," says the smiling, scrawny boy. "Unless you want to wait until it arrives."

"How long do you expect," I ask.

"The fuel truck was supposed to be here at 11 o'clock," he replies.

I glance at my watch. It's now 12:15.

"Is there a place I can park for lunch? Maybe the gas will be here when I come back."

"Sure. Move your boat around to that dock, behind the metal boat," he says, pointing to a narrow row with boats parked tight and parallel.

"I'll check in with you when I get back from lunch," I say. "Maybe you can help me over there. Looks tight for an amateur like me."

"Sure. I'll meet you there."

Moving the boat around is easy. Getting into the avenue of water between the docks is also simple, but getting out will not be. When I notice the blond boy already positioned to assist with my lines, I'm pleased.

"Since you're here, how about helping me get turned around?" I yell down to him from the command bridge.

"Kinda narrow here. Do you have enough room to turn around?"

"With your help. It's better than having to back out. Better for your marina, too."

The boy smiles back at me, ready to grab my bow rail as I swing around. He can act as the pivot point for my boat, and I'll assist with the engine. The boat clears all sides during the course reversal by only a few feet, with the stern-drive leg riding up close to the dock as I turn. But it works, and I'm safely docked. Best of all, I can drive forward and out, a much easier exit.

I have lunch in the outdoor patio area at the Heriot Bay Inn. They have omelets all-day, a nice surprise. It's the first cup of coffee I've had in several days, and it's a delicious brunch treat. Afterwards, I visit the inn's gift shop, where I meet Juanita.

"I bet you'd appreciate the short version of my sales pitch," I say, as I lay some of my books on the counter.

"Sure would," says Juanita. "It's been that kind of a day."

Juanita has her hand in everything at the inn, but right now she's trying to simultaneously break in a new gift shop employee and assist at the lodging desk. She buys some of my books and expresses the kind of enthusiasm for local authors (not so local here) that's always appreciated.

When I get back to the dock, the fuel has arrived, but it hasn't yet been pumped down from the truck positioned in the parking lot

above the gas dock. That process seems to be in progress, or at least about to begin. Meanwhile, boaters are waiting for gas, and I'd rather not be a part of the queue.

"I'm back," I tell the gas boy, who is trying to please everyone, an impossible task without fuel. "I'll wait in my boat until the others get their gas."

I'd like to think I've taken a little of the pressure off this lad. Yet, he seems to like the excitement of all of the people on his dock. A woman in shorts and T-shirt sits patiently next to the pump with a cruise-a-day tank. Two men in a runabout are parked at the pumps, looking less patient. On the VHF radio in the background, I hear a boater asking if fuel is available yet.

I stretch out in a canvas lawn chair in the back of the Bayliner, reading a copy of *Wavelength*, a kayak magazine that I found in the gift shop. After a few minutes, just when the fuel seems to finally be available, *Footloose*, a 40-foot maroon-and-white American Tug, enters the harbour and demands immediate attention by her mere size. The gas boy jogs from the pumps to the slip where the big boat is destined, the dock-finger next to me. As the teenager assists with the docking, the boat's captain wants to discuss his overnight arrangements, disregarding the people waiting at the pump. I can feel the tension in the air, and I'm glad I'm not a part of it. It's a fine day for reading a magazine on the aft deck.

All settles down in a surprisingly short time. The woman with the cruise-a-day gets her gas, the men in the runabout are gone, and *Footloose*'s crew have gone to shore. I walk back to the shack near the pumps and poke my head inside. The young lad is frantically punching at a calculator, probably trying to make the frenzied activity of the past half-hour balance in his fuel records.

"I'm ready, if I can bring my boat around now," I say.

"Sure! We'll finally get you some gas."

It's a fairly easy exit from my parking spot, nearly straight ahead since I'm already turned around. Still, since I insist on giving the boat in front of me lots of clearance, I manage to bump against the far side of the dock. The scrape doesn't seem significant, but it gets the attention of a boater a few spots in front of me. Apparently, he felt the bump, causing him to suddenly appear on the flying bridge of his big yacht.

"Can I give you some help?" he asks, probably planning to hop down and stand ready to protect his boat.

"No, I've got 'er now," I say, speaking nearly face-to-face to him from my command bridge. "I just like to hit a few docks on the way out."

"Okay," he says.

I don't think he's laughing, particularly since his boat is in my line of travel. But I make my exit without any further excitement.

At the gas dock, I take on 140 litres, all in the main tank. Before starting the engine, I flip the fuel tank switch from *Main* to *Aux*. I seldom use my auxiliary fuel, and its good to burn up that gas once in a while. Old gas isn't a major problem, but it's best replaced with fresh fuel every few months.

The delay in getting fuel has allowed me time to study the charts. There are several promising anchorages just a few kilometres north of Heriot Bay. One of them, Moulds Bay, looks particularly interesting, although it probably can handle only a few boats swinging on anchor. If this bay proves crowded, I'll simply continue north until I find a place where I can comfortably fit and still maintain some privacy.

It's barely worth coming up on-plane for the trip to Moulds Bay, so I plow along at a semi-planing speed of 15 knots. In just a few minutes, I navigate behind Breton Island and get a clear view of the bay. The only boat in sight is stern-lined to shore, a good distance from the spot on my map that looks best for anchoring.

My anchor goes down and grabs efficiently on the first try. I shut off the engine and settle in for a relaxing afternoon.

As the tide rolls into Moulds Bay, the sky becomes more thickly covered by mid-level clouds, but there's no rain. The temperature is 22 degrees, which I consider perfect. On the VHF, the marine weather report confirms that the low pressure system has moved onto the Oregon coast. The bad weather is focused well to the south, and expected to remain that way well into tomorrow. Overcast skies, mild temperature, and light winds are perfect news for me.

Moulds Bay is a fine spot for exploration by dinghy, but I elect to stay aboard the Bayliner and simply relax. I'm satisfied on my aft deck, just reading and occasionally listening to the FM radio. However, there's one task that still hasn't been accomplished on this trip. I've brought along a gallon of antifreeze, intending to add it to the heat exchanger during one of my overnight stops. Last month, I replaced the Bayliner's water hoses during maintenance on the cooling system, after an incident involving overheating (see the previous chapter). Lots of antifreeze was lost in the process. I'm really not sure how much was lost, and I've been unable to determine from my boat manual the total capacity of the fresh-water cooling system. But I know I'm now deficient in anti-freeze. So there's no time like the present to take care of the task.

First, I must make room for the antifreeze, so I siphon the contents of the heat exhanger reservoir into a bucket. Then I detach one end of the cooling hose, capturing a little more liquid. In total, my bucket holds only 2 litres of fluid, well below the capacity of the cooling system, but I've created enough space for an adequate dose of fresh antifreeze. I reattach the hose and fill the reservoir with the green liquid from the gallon container.

I make a mental note to recheck the fluid level at my next stop. It's a comfortable feeling to know I'm finally getting a mechanical feel for this boat. It's been a slow process, but doing some of my own maintenance leaves me with a more secure feeling when at sea. I might not be able to handle a major mechanical problem on my own, but at least I've become familiar with the subsystems over time.

Which leads to an unusual place to end this chapter. Yet, what happens to my boat next deserves a chapter of its own, so read on…

Chapter 7

Flameout

Moulds Bay on Quadra Island is a wonderful anchorage, more so on this particular afternoon when I'm alone in this peaceful spot. The other boat in this bay, a small private trawler, is far enough away to make me feel isolated. It's a great feeling.

As high tide approaches, seaweed lazily drifts past the Bayliner and towards shore. I sit on the aft deck, reading an old Farley Mowat book and sipping a cold 7-Up with the luxury of ice that's still available from my departure from Powell River yesterday.

Clunk! – what was that? It's more than a small piece of driftwood hitting the boat, but not enough to incite concern. Still, what hit the hull?

While still sitting in my canvas chair, I lean over the stern on the starboard side. Nothing there.

Then I stand and look back over the dinghy, *Mr. Bathtub*, and farther rearward. Nothing there either.

Walking to the port side, I'm startled to find a huge log gently brushing the whole left side of the boat, pushed shoreward by the high tide. This is no small piece of timber – about 10 metres long, cut at both ends, and nearly a metre in diameter. There's no damage to the boat, a mere bump, but what a big log to flow in on high tide, probably broken loose from a towed boom.

Slack water is approaching, typically a good time to catch fish. Of course, I'm in only 30-feet of water, but it's worth a try. I cast my lure towards deeper water. I jig a few times and start to rewind my line. Right away I catch a fish – a small flounder. I'm surprised to catch a flounder in this shallow spot, particularly since I expect the bottom to be mud or rocky, rather than sand or gravel. In fact, I'm surprised to catch anything at all.

Two casts later, I get another strike, this time considerably larger than the flounder. But within a few winds of my reel, the fish is gone.

After a few more casts, something large hits my lure. The fight is on, and it's a nice battle. It's large enough for a salmon, but finding a salmon here seems illogical. I caught one in shallow water in Bute Inlet, but this is a long way from Bute. Still, this fish fights strong, and it might be a salmon.

When I get the fish near the surface, but still too deep to see, it darts under the boat. I try to pull it back quickly, since it seems headed for the prop. I win the battle and wrestle my prize towards the surface. Now I see it clearly, and it's a salmon. No, it's a dogfish – a very big dogfish (shark), and I've snagged it well behind its mouth. I ponder how I'll get the lure unhooked, and I imagine the 3-foot dogfish snapping its ugly teeth around to grab my hand. Or its spiked tail could whip around to gash me.

With the fish at the surface, its weight is even more pronounced. My pole bends in a steep arch, and I shake the rod, trying to free the lure. This isn't a situation where I desire to reach down towards the fish with my pliers. Suddenly, in answer to my hopes, the dogfish flops violently, the lure breaks loose, and the shark plops solidly back into the water and is gone.

No more fishing here today. It was a fun fight, but I'm glad it's over, with the dogfish back down to the bottom. I'm content sitting on the aft deck, reading and enjoying the quieter aspects of life.

As the day draws to an end, I climb up to the command bridge and snap a self-portrait of a solo voyager in a remarkably uncrowded anchorage at the end of a pleasant July day.

* * * * *

The next morning dawns cloudy, cool, and calm. I plan to return to Powell River this morning, so I'll get breakfast there. I spend a few minutes tidying up the cabin so there'll be little to do when I return to Westview Harbour. I tune in the marine weather report, which promises continued excellent conditions on the chuck until late afternoon. By sunset, rain is expected.

In preparation for raising the anchor, I open the engine hatch to switch the batteries from the *#1* overnight setting to *Both* for engine start. I close the hatch and climb up to the command bridge. I turn on the blower, wait a few seconds, and crank the starter. It's not a smooth start, requiring more pumps of the throttle than are usually necessary, but the engine runs smoothly once it gets going. The engine hasn't been starting well lately, but it's hardly worth worrying about. I raise the anchor and start for home.

This morning, I cruise on the auxiliary tank, knowing it'll last only 45 minutes. My plan is to run the aux tank dry, or nearly so, before switching back to the main tank again. If I'm quick enough, I may be able to catch the engine when it begins to sputter dry and switch to the main tank before the motor quits. At the next refuel, I'll pump fresh fuel into the aux tank, ready to sit there for another few months.

As I pass Rebecca Spit (Drew Bay), I consider the scenarios regarding the aux tank. Should I use this tank until it's completely empty, with the risk of flameout that will require a restart? And can't you pick up contaminants from the bottom of an empty tank. Then there's the problem of having to restart an engine at sea. Even when I fish in the ocean, I usually keep the engine running to avoid the necessity of restarting the motor. After all, starters can fail, and a thousand other things can go wrong when you try to start an engine. I could solve all of these potential problems by simply running the fuel until the gauge says the aux tank is nearly empty, and then switch over to the main tank. Better yet, I could use the elapsed time, since boat fuel gauges are notoriously inaccurate.

However, I'm alone on the boat today, driving from the command bridge, and there's no fuel gauge and tank selection switch here. To go downstairs when alone on this boat requires coming off-plane, reducing power to idle (preferably neutral), and then going down to the cabin to check the fuel gauge or change the tank. So it's partly a matter of efficiency.

What I finally decide to do is use time to tell me when I'm near empty. Then, keeping my hand on the throttle, I'll be ready to come back to idle promptly when the engine first sputters. I might be able to make it downstairs and switch to the main tank before the engine quits. If I'm trying to get rid of old fuel in the aux tank, it's the best way to get rid of the most gas.

For now, there's no concern. I'm cruising along nicely, still at least 30 minutes before the aux tanks goes empty, and it's a gorgeous day. "Gorgeous," of course, is in the eyes of the beholder. For me, smooth sea conditions are gorgeous, regardless of the sky conditions. The mid-level clouds threaten rain, mostly to the south, and the cool temperature requires a jacket on the command bridge. I simply love it.

Off to the left is Cortes Island, now slipping quickly behind. Next is Hernando, then Savary, Harwood, and home. But the biggest island of all in front of me, still far to the south, is Texada. Powell River is off the north tip of Texada Island, so I'll not pass it on this trip, but already it looms large on the horizon.

Now at mid-tide, a long line of rocks extends outward from the southwest tip of Cortes, a hazard that deserves a wide berth. Fortunately, with a GPS, the rock obstacles are easily avoided. I round the last of the rocks and focus on Hernando Island to the left of the bow. Farther in front, Texada now takes on the shape of a whale's tail, thrust towards the west. I used to think it looked like a crouching elephant, but time and environment change the way you think.

The moment is near, and my hand is on the throttle. The Bayliner cruises nicely on-plane along the west side of Hernando, and then the engine sputters.

I catch it immediately, throttling full back, and then shift into neutral. The engine is purring smoothly at idle. I hustle down to the aft deck and swing on a pivot foot into the cabin. Down two more steps and forward to the captain's chair. Without sitting down, I flip the fuel switch from *Aux* to *Main*, and the engine continues to run. Made it!

Although the waves are not large, there are some moderate swells, and I feel them more down here than on the command bridge. It's okay for a few minutes, but I wouldn't like to put up with it for long. But I could use a bathroom break while I'm here, so I use the opportunity to step into the head. Immediately the engine quits.

It's no surprise. It could've been a fuel bubble, churned up as I switched tanks; or even a bit of contamination from the bottom of the aux tank or some water that was trapped there. But it should be an easy process to restart the engine.

I climb back up to the command bridge and sit down in front of the control wheel. This should be a hot start, so I leave the throttle at idle and engage the starter, but the engine cranks over but does not start. I try pumping the throttle and cranking the starter again, but to no avail. Now I wonder if I've flooded the engine. Rather than risk killing the batteries, I decide to wait a few minutes for an overprimed carburetor to settle.

Waiting brings no resolution to my starting problem. I try starting the engine again, but still no results. I've been cranking long enough now to begin worrying about the batteries. Just as that thought surfaces, on the next attempt to start the engine, the batteries die. I engage the starter and it simply clicks.

Hernando Island is about two kilometres to the east, and Mitlenatch Island is directly to the west, considerably farther. In an instant, I go from mildly concerned to heart-thumping anxious. Not only have I lost my engine, I've also killed my batteries. Will there even be enough electrical power to operate my VHF radio? I'm not adverse to calling the Coast Guard, but I'll need electrons to do it.

I still have my cell phone, but will it work in this location? I click it on – *Extended Service* with one bar. Then I think of something that seems futile, but it's worth checking. I climb down from the command bridge and swing the engine compartment hatch upward to fully expose the engine. I lean over the edge of the compartment and look down at the battery switch. Miracle! – the switch is positioned on *#1*, which means my biggest battery is still in reserve. How did this happen, and why did I even consider checking this switch now? When I anchor overnight, I routinely switch from *Both* to *#1* to isolate the electrical system for night use. That assures I'll have electrical power in the morning for the engine start, even if I abuse the use of electricity during the night. In the morning, before starting the engine, I switch back to *Both*, and off I go. Apparently, I didn't perform this routine action at Moulds Bay this morning.

Yet, I specifically remember going through the habitual action. I'm certain I raised the compartment hatch, and I even remember touching the battery switch. But the switch now sits in *#1* position, so obviously something wasn't routine. In any case, I've been granted a second chance, although the switch's position strikes me as a bit spooky.

I move the battery switch to *Both*, leave the engine compartment cover open, and take my cell phone up to the command bridge. I plan to take full advantage of my second chance, and a call to John is a wise first step. There are several possibilities regarding this situation. Starting has been difficult in recent weeks, but it hasn't been enough to seem of concern, until now. A flameout when pulling into the harbour at Lund two days ago now rings clear. That sudden engine stoppage at idle was unusual, and was probably related to what's happening today.

Running the auxiliary tank dry may be part of the equation – maybe the engine stopped only because of an air bubble, but more likely water or contamination in the bottom of the tank was drawn into the fuel lines. There's a fuel filter somewhere, but I'm not familiar with its location.

There's also the possibility the fuel tank selector switch (an electrical toggle switch) could be broken. If so, I'm still on the aux tank, and it's empty. I know there's plenty of gas in the main tank, but that makes little difference if I can't get at it. One thing seems certain about the source of the problem – it's fuel, fuel, or fuel.

From the command bridge, I dial John's phone number, and Ed answers. He reports that John just left the house to go up the lake. Rick is driving his taxi cab this morning, so maybe I can reach him on his cell phone. I ring the number, and Rick answers on the second ring.

"Can you talk now," I ask, knowing he's in his cab.

"For a minute," says Rick.

"I've had a flameout in the Bayliner. Can't get the engine started. Doesn't even seem to fire."

"Where are you?" asks Rick.

"Between Hernando Island and Mitlenatch."

"Are you serious?"

"I'm afraid so. I was running on the aux tank, and ran it dry. Now the engine won't fire on the main tank, which is full of gas."

"Sounds like the fuel filter," says Rick. "Oh, wait. Here's John."

I hear voices in the background. Then John comes on the line.

"Where are you?" I ask.

"At the Shinglemill," says John. "Just pulled in, and Rick was sitting here."

Powell River is a mighty small world.

"Did Rick tell you what's happened to my engine?" I ask.

"A little. Try cleaning out the fuel filter."

"Where is it?"

"I'm not sure, but you can trace it easy. Just find the line coming out of the tank. It looks like an oil filter, but a little smaller. It's between the tank and the engine. Oh, Rick's gotta go now."

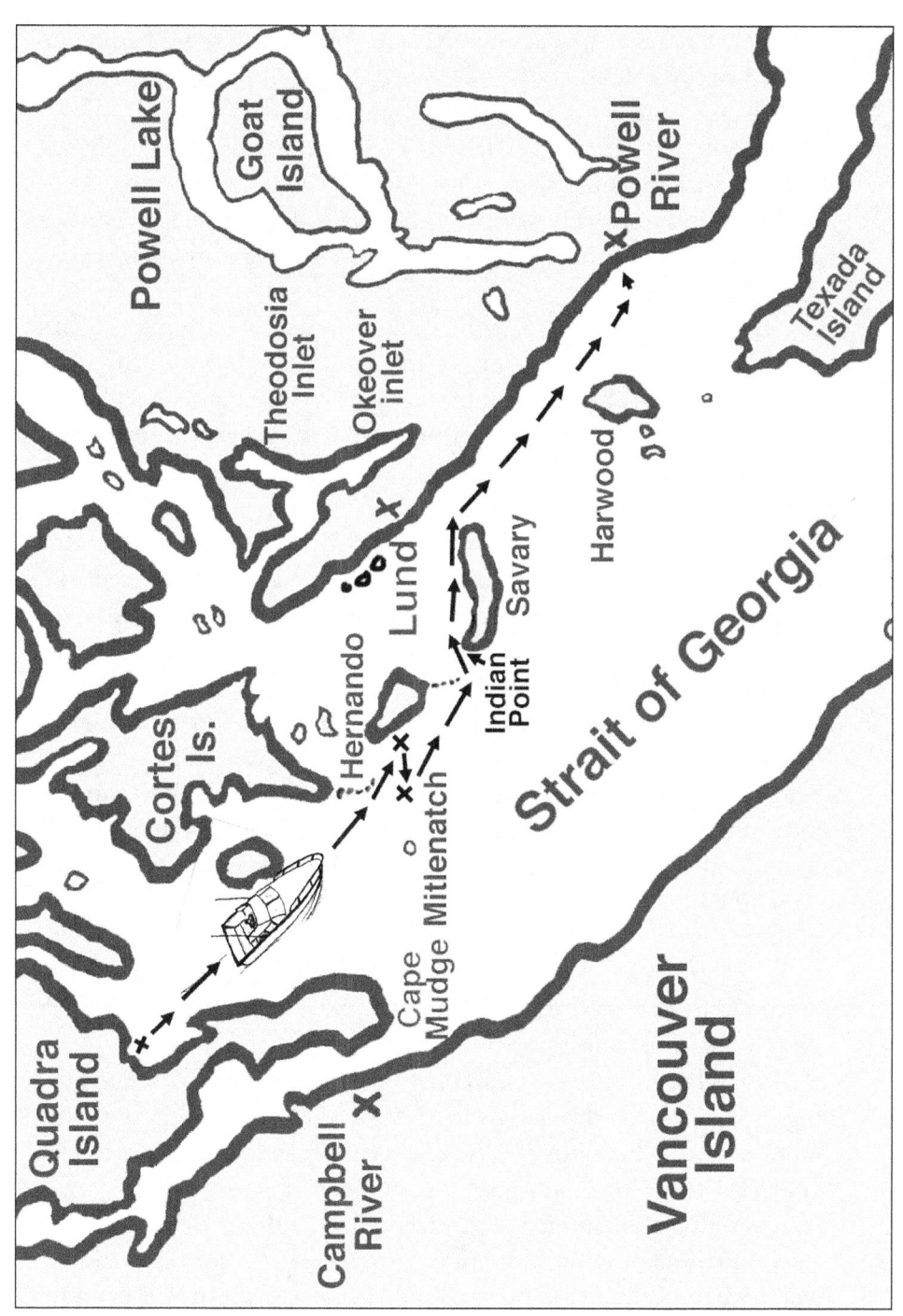

"Hey, can I call you back somewhere? Maybe you should go home, and I'll call you there."

"I'll go to a phone booth. What's your number?"

"I'm not sure that will work. It's a U.S. number, and a phone booth will take a ton of coins."

"Rick's in a hurry. He just got a radio call for a pickup. Call my dad, and I'll keep in touch with him. But try the fuel filter first. Gotta go."

Click.

It all makes sense. The fuel filter is probably plugged with contaminants from the bottom of the aux tank, preventing any flow to the engine. Probably the filter was already starting to clog before today, just the normal course of things. That would explain the recent hard starts and the flameout at Lund. Today was simply the last straw. Maybe this is going to be simple, after all.

I go back down to the engine compartment and find the fuel line coming out of the engine. I trace it to a bulkhead, only a few feet from the battery switch. The filter is out of sight unless you crane your neck under the lip of the engine compartment. It looks like a small, green oil filter, mounted vertically, with a knurled knob at the bottom. I grab the knob, expecting it to be rusted shut, but I'm able to twist it open with my fingers. A small spurt of fuel gushes out – opaque, reddish-yellow gas with small blobs of a black solid gunk. It's only a few grams, not nearly the capacity of the filter. I tap on the filter, and some more drops trickle out, along with a few more pieces of black crud. The filter seems plugged, and that gives me hope I've found the problem.

I try unscrewing the filter from its mount, but it's John-tight, enhanced by at least a year's exposure to salt water corrosion. I wrench on it some more, but it doesn't budge.

While I'm in the cabin searching through my tools for something big enough to grab the entire filter and twist it loose, I feel the rolling motion of the boat. In the now increasing swells, that motion is enhanced inside the cabin, and I feel a momentary touch of sea sickness. If the swells get much bigger, this could be a problem for me.

I don't find anything big enough to grab the whole filter, so I try wrapping some duct tape around it, leaving an extra foot to pull on for increased torque. The filter doesn't budge.

Knowing it has been long enough for a flooded carburetor to take care of itself, I try starting the engine again. Maybe the small amount of contaminate drained from the small plug has resolved the situation. But again, the engine fails to start.

Among the thoughts going through my mind is a suspicion the throttle may not be priming the engine when I pump it, although it has always done so in the past. Could that be the source of my problem rather than a contaminated fuel filter or a flooded carburetor?

I remove the air filter from the top of the carburetor, so I can see the throttle valves. With the engine compartment open and the air filter removed, I can look down on the butterfly valves from the command bridge. So I pump the throttle while looking down at the carburetor. There are two big throttle valves at the rear and a narrow valve at the front. The front valve moves a small amount when I pump the throttle, but neither of the big valves budge, and that doesn't seem right. (I later learn it's normal during engine start.)

I use the cell phone to call Ed. John is still not home and hasn't checked in since I talked to him at the Shinglemill. I tell Ed about my concerns regarding the throttle linkage.

"Well, if you're not sure it's getting fuel, you could pour some gas into the carburetor as you try to start it," he says.

"I thought about that," I say (which is true). "Should I use about a cup of gas?"

"No, no! Not that much. Just a tablespoon or so. You don't want to start a fire."

No, I don't want to start a fire. Maybe I should try something else first.

Ed recommends trying a piece of rope on the fuel filter.

"Make a couple of half-hitches, to draw the knot real tight," he says. "And leave a long piece so you can put some knots in it for a good grip."

"I'll give it a try," I say.

I'm terrible with knots. A half-hitch means nothing to me, but I manage to get a tight knot around the filter. Then I crawl down into the engine compartment to get a better angle on my pull. At first nothing, than I feel a bit of give, followed by a loud *Crack!* as the entire filter assembly, including the mounting bracket, pops out of the bulkhead. Three big mounting screws have pulled loose, along with a few chips of wood. John isn't going to like this!

With the entire filter assembly in my hands, I try again to unscrew the filter from its mount. Maybe if I tap on the mount with a hammer while holding the filter tight, it'll loosen. *Whack! Whack! Zing!* – a chunk of the mount casting, including one of the three screw holes, breaks off and falls to the bottom of the bilge. John is definitely not going to be pleased.

I give up on loosening the filter, but maybe it'll help to remove the two port plugs on the mount. There are four ports, but only two are connected to hoses (one from the tank and one leading to the engine). I surmise that the remaining two ports, although unused in this installation, will give me access to the inside of the filter. Surprisingly, I'm able to break the two plugs loose, and I pry down inside the filter with a coat hanger. I'm sure this isn't an approved process, and it's possible I'll damage the filter and make things worse. Then again, things can't get much worse.

I can't get the coat hanger far enough inside the filter to do anything. But I could pour gas into the ports, slosh it around, and pour it out. I could, that is, if I had any gas. The outboard kicker's gas can is (was) stored in the head, but when I open the door, it's gone. I search every conceivable place in the boat, and there's no gas can. But I'm able to drain enough gas from the kicker's tank (which is nearly empty) to slosh through the filter ports. I decide to repeat the process a few more times, including tapping on the filter with a hammer, since each time more black particles come out.

While I go through this process, I consider a few things. First, I wonder if sloshing with gas that has been mixed with oil for the two-stroke kicker is a bad thing. I conclude it's a minor concern. Second, and much closer to the front of my mind, is the kicker itself. It's only a 3-horsepower outboard intended for the dinghy, but I once practiced mounting it on the transom and using it to propel the Bayliner for a short distance, in calm conditions. The kicker might keep me off the rocks in near-perfect conditions, but it certainly isn't designed for a long trip to shore. Still, until now, it was a comforting thought to know it was aboard. But today, without fuel, it will be useless. (Hopefully, if I had decided I needed to use the kicker, I would've considered siphoning fuel from the Bayliner's gas tank. Admittedly, at the time, that did not occur to me.)

Now finished with the sloshing process, I reinstall the port plugs and strap the filter and its mount to the fuel tank with some duct tape. Then I climb back up onto the command bridge and try to start the engine. This time, it fires momentarily, but I can't keep the engine running. I try again and again. Each time I'm encouraged by a brief firing of the spark plugs that causes the engine to run briefly, then die.

I try starting the engine while pumping the throttle repeatedly, and the engine fires again, this time when the throttle is fully advanced. I decide to try leaving the throttle full forward, although that can't be good for the engine. But now it's running, barely so, popping and backfiring. I still refuse to retard the throttle, even though the engine begins to rev up. Finally, when the engine is turning at nearly full power, I pull the throttle back slowly, and the motor runs wonderfully smooth at low (but not yet idle) power.

"Hurrah!" I yell.

It doesn't matter that there's no one but me to hear.

I look back down into the engine compartment. I don't normally see the engine when it's running, and now I see something that shocks me. A tiny squirt of water is streaming from the end of the heat exchanger – not a gushing stream, but more like a squirt gun. Then the spray of water stops.

With the motor still running at low power, I climb down to the engine compartment and look for further loss of water. I don't see any fluid exiting the reservoir now, but when I reach down to carefully touch the area where the squirt originated (it's warm, not hot), the metal is wet. Not gushing wet, but dripping. Maybe at low power (and low temperatures), I'll be able to limp home.

After the engine has run smoothly at its low throttle setting for a few minutes, I'm brave enough to come all the way back to idle and shift into forward gear.

"We're off!"

I speak to myself, like I need to tell someone all is okay again. I may have a new problem (coolant leak), but I'm glad to have an engine, even if it may not get me all the way home.

I advance the throttle a little, but I'm concerned with what may be inadequate fuel flow through the filter at a higher power setting,

coupled with a coolant leak. I settle into a 5 knot crawl towards the passage between Hernando and Savary Island. There are a lot of rocks extending out from Hernando Island, so I check the GPS and give them a wide berth.

"Hey, Ed!" I nearly yell into the phone. "I've got 'er running!"

It's nice to have someone to share my success with. I tell Ed I'm afraid to add too much power, and he agrees. When he hears about my coolant leak, he reminds me its particularly important to take it slow.

"Keep an eye on that leak the best you can," he suggests. "Keep the power back, and the engine should be okay."

I'm now well past the last rock sticking out from Hernando, and make the turn between the islands. I parallel Savary, passing a few hundred metres off Indian Point, where several boats are moored. When I look ahead to the far end of the island, I begin to reevaluate my speed. I've never traveled very far in a boat at 5 knots, and I'm not known for my patience. I rationalize that the engine is now running fine. I have already paid two more visits to the engine compartment, and the coolant leak is still only a few drips. So I push the power up a bit, determine from my GPS that my speed is now 8 knots, and settle in for a slow cruise back to Powell River.

Within another half kilometre, it begins to rain. At first, it's only a light splattering of drops. But it quickly increases to a mild downpour. A cool wind whips up, felt more distinctly at this slow speed. Here on the command bridge, I take the brunt of the rain. It would be a lot more pleasant in the cabin below. I could drive from there, but visibility is so much better up here. Yet, I'm beginning to get drenched.

Down I go, checking the coolant leak (still barely noticeable) on the way into the cabin. I settle into the captain's chair and am shocked by the poor visibility. This isn't the first time I've driven from this position, but it's the first time I've driven from here at 8 knots. Since I'm plowing water, rather than on-plane, I can barely see over the bow. If there are any logs in front of me in these waves, I'll never see them. Visibility would be so much better on-plane.

I push the throttle up, finally settling in at 15 knots, a little below my normal cruising speed. It's enough of a power reduction below standard that the engine seems to labor less. Yet, I'm making comfortable forward progress.

I slip around the Lund-end of Savary, and start down the coast towards Powell River. In a few minutes, I'll be closer to Powell River than Lund. If the engine quits then, I'll be in the jurisdiction of Powell River's Coast Guard. Getting a tow to the nearest port will mean a tow to Westview Harbour, which is home.

The rain continues, and the engine performs smoothly. Westview Harbour is a wonderful sight.

There's something about getting through this incident and home on my own power that gives me great satisfaction. I'm quick to admit I'm mechanically challenged, but I persevered today, and it worked out in the end. And I learned a lot in the process. It's the kind of experience that gives you confidence in yourself. And it makes you appreciate the always dominant power of the sea.

* * * * *

Afterwards:

John is not happy with my damage to the fuel filter mount, but he's glad I was able to limp back to Westview Harbour. When John disassembles the filter, even he struggles to remove it, but the cause of my flameout is then obvious. Considerable contamination has been drawn through the filter, then downstream into the smaller engine-mounted filter, enough to shut off the flow of fuel to the engine. The bottom of the auxiliary tank was contaminated with a mix of particulates (which now have, hopefully, been mostly withdrawn from the tank). How the stuff got into the tank is not so clear. When we eventually change the engine the next year, we find considerable water in the auxiliary tank that could easily entrap contaminants. We conclude that the water may have gotten into the tank through the gas cap vent.

◊ ◊ ◊ ◊ ◊ ◊ ◊

Chapter 8

Squirrel Cove

The water is about as rough as I find acceptable, with two to three-foot seas and quite a bit of whacking on the hull. Margy and I slowly cross the open stretch north of Sarah Point en route to Squirrel Cove. The clouds are supposed to clear later today, and the mid-June temperature should rise to 20. The next frontal impulse is supposed to hold off until tomorrow afternoon.

The Squirrel Cove wharf finally appears (it always seems to take longer in rough water) around the point. The docks seem to nearly touch the shore at this low tide. Few boats are tied here today. There's even a spot on the outermost finger where the water is the deepest, but it looks tight. With today's moderate wind pushing us, I'd prefer a wide-open spot. So I slip around the first dock, intending to tie up on the backside, where the row is open except for one sailboat. But, as I round the corner, I'm pushed out of position by the wind. So now I change my mind and aim for the outside of the next dock. It's a good choice, with plenty of depth and no other boats to contend with during docking. The Bayliner drifts shoreward and bumps against the dock with a gentle thump. John would be proud of me.

It's a steep climb up the ramp at low tide, but with a great view from above. The boats lie below, with the Squirrel Cove general store and shops spreading north of the wharf. In the parking lot of the store, next to the gas pump, is an old school bus, uniquely adapted for island travel. The sides are painted in a rough psychedelic design, and a pile of trash (or valuables) is strapped to the roof. From this distance, I can see the rooftop hosts a bicycle (or maybe just its tire), a lot of wound rope, and a mix of who-knows-what.

Margy and I walk past the store on the way to the cafe. From close-up, the bus is quite a sight. The mound of stuff on the roof is now more easily identified. It's a pile you might find at your local dump, only more organized. As I inspect the bus closer, a thirty-ish couple exits the general store. They are immediately identifiable as the owners of this classic vehicle. The man has a long beard and broad brimmed hat. He wears a white T-shirt, long jeans (honest-to-goodness bell-bottoms), and sandals. The young woman accompanying him is wearing a dull blue granny dress, and she's clutching a black plastic bottle of motor oil. In fact, she's rubbing the bottle against her cheek, kissing and talking to it.

We slow our pace to take in the unique scene. While the couple boards their bus, a blue pickup truck arrives and a silver SUV departs from the parking lot. Nobody seems to pay any attention to the bus. I conclude it is recognized by all but us. Locals right out of the 60's. I do the math – they must be reliving an era that ended well before they were born.

The bus pulls away, its engine pinging loudly during its climb to the main road. Maybe they should have added the oil before starting the engine.

Margy and I continue to the nearby cafe, passing the dinghy dock that's closer to the store and small shops but unusable at low tide. When I say "unusable," I speak in the strictest sense. It's fully landlocked at low tide. The entire dock now sits about 50 feet inland, with a tin boat and its outboard motor bobbing in the completed surrounded pool of water.

At the curve in the road, it becomes obvious that the cafe isn't open. The tables and chairs on the deck are stacked, and the building is dark. There's no sign on the door indicating hours of operation – maybe not even open yet for the summer season. Like a lot of marine-dependent businesses in the region, mid-June isn't considered summer. It's all or none in this area – you're either open full-bore for the season or you're closed down tight. Until the kids are out of school, it's definitely not summer.

Margy and I aren't surprised to find the cafe closed. We weren't depending on it for today's main meal. We have plenty of junk food (our favourite on-the-hook menu), but it would be nice to have a full meal tonight. So we decide to give the general store a try.

It's a small store, but there's a wide variety of merchandise. Not a lot of anything, but like most general stores, a bit of everything. There's an additional room with marine gear, but no fresh or frozen meat except for hot dogs and shrink-wrapped chunks of ground beef shaped like hamburger patties. We decide the Bayliner's store-bought pizza and potato salad, along with our multitude of snacks, will be plenty for tonight's supper.

After we leave the store, Margy comments about the lack of fresh meat. This is one of the major stores on this large island.

"Maybe we should have asked about the meat. Maybe they keep it behind the counter or something."

"Like cigarettes, out of the reach of minors," I quip. "Or maybe it was in the walk-in locker, although the label on the door indicated it contained fruits and eggs."

It's not important enough to go back to to check again, so we keep walking. Soon we're back at the wharf. We descend the steep ramp to the docks and depart for the other Squirrel Cove, the one where we'll anchor.

In fact, there are really three Squirrel Coves: the wharf and village of shops, the nearby First Nations town on the side of the hill, and the anchorage. Each is called Squirrel Cove, but everybody knows the difference. I didn't the first time I visited several years ago. When I arrived at the wharf, I couldn't figure out why it looked so different from my boating guide's diagram of the anchorage. Then I realized I missed my destination by several kilometres.

The waves have subsided a bit, and the short trip to the other Squirrel Cove (the anchorage) is comfortable. We follow a sailboat into the narrow but deep entrance.

Like other places in this region in mid-June, the anchorage has lots of room to spare. The wide bay inside the entrance isn't the favourite anchoring spot for many, but it's the location of Marilyn's Salmon Shack. I deviate to the left to pass near the shed-like building not much bigger than a hotdog stand, just in case Marilyn is open early.

Highly unlikely. There's a tin boat at Marilyn's dock, but no sign of life near the shack.

A single sailboat is anchored in the large bay, and a surprising number of boats occupy the primary anchorage farther in. It's a respectable number for this time of year. I count 19 boats at anchor in a cove that will hold 50 or more in another three weeks. Today, there's plenty of remaining space to swing on anchor, without the need for a stern line. We choose a spot near the small island where you always see a boater walking a dog. I call it Dog Poop Island.

We drop anchor midway between the island and the promontory at the cove's other entrance, a shallow channel that's only usable by small boats. We're near the floating bakery (closed, of course), which has been freshly painted pale blue. This on-and-off-again bakery is a very popular spot for boaters during the summer. There's enough business from those anchored to provide the baker with a healthy summer income.

Next to the bakery, a large commercial fishing boat, *Good Hope No. 2*, has dropped anchored in what looks like a permanent spot. It's an impressive vessel whose size exceeds the entire bakery.

For the rest of the day, we sit on *Halcyon Day's* aft deck, reading and listening to the radio. A cool southeast breeze slinks into the cove, pushing us gently on our anchor, but this is a well-protected spot, even if the approaching storm moves in earlier than forecast. By late afternoon, the sky darkens, with windswept high clouds indicating the weather is about to change. I dial in the marine forecast on the boat's VHF and am pleased to learn the approaching low is still well off the northern tip of Vancouver Island.

I use a plastic bucket to skim the surface for a water sample for my microscope. This is a well-trodden cove, so it will be difficult to distinguish the natural critters from those left by man's gray water, but it's worth a try. That's the nice thing about swinging on the hook – you have time to squander.

I let the water settle in the bucket for about an hour and then transfer a sample to a small bottle. After another hour, using an eyedropper, I draw a few drops from the bottom of the bottle to assure I'm getting the most settled part of the sample. I place two drops on a slide that has a concave recess and add a cover slip. Then I put the slide under the microscope, flip on the built-in light, and select the lens with lowest magnification.

There's a lot to see in the binocular eyepieces. Even at low magnification, there's the usual overwhelming bits of debris, probably mostly contaminants, but a lot of plant life as well. Gray-green algae blobs form rough circles. Other green and reddish-brown sinuous threads are clear signs of chloroplasts.

I move around the slide by adjusting the microscope's knurled knobs. Suddenly an animal-like organism shoots into view. It moves fast, but I'm able to watch it long enough before it departs the field of view to verify it has a flagellum. I try to find the critter again by adjusting the mechanical stage to view other parts of the slide. I don't find the organism again, nor do I find any other signs of animal life on the slide during my half-hour at the scope.

A few hours later, I drop the Kemmerer bottle over the side of the Bayliner to collect a deeper water sample. I drop into 40 feet of water using a 5-pound weight and 3/8th-inch rope.

When the weight reaches the bottom, it transfers an obvious thump up the rope to my hand. I visualize the bottle hanging vertically a metre above the cove's floor. Now I snap the messenger weight to the line and drop it. In a few seconds, my hand detects another fainter but distinct thump. I raise the bottle to the surface (40 feet of hand-

over-hand pulling), resulting in a tangle of yellow rope on the deck. I extract a sample from the Kemmerer drain tube into a small bottle.

After letting the sample settle and using the same eyedropper technique, I examine the results under the microscope. This time there are no animal organisms visible, nor is there as much algae. Compared to the surface sample, the slide is nearly empty. How much of the difference is due to fewer contaminants? – an interesting (and unanswered) question. Still, there's plenty on the slide to attract my attention for the next few minutes. I examine the sample thoroughly, and come away with the conclusion it's similar to the surface water but less teeming with life.

Near sunset, two large powerboats pull into the cove nearly simultaneously. One slides behind Dog Poop Island and then returns to anchor near us. The other stops in the deeper water of the entry bay.

"They're here!" yells Margy, in a tone that tells me exactly what she means.

A U.S. flag flies on the stern of both boats. The Americans are moving north in their annual migration up the Strait of Georgia. Summer cannot be far behind.

In the evening twilight, Canadian geese fly back and forth over the cove, low-level formations only a few metres above the water. One flock of about ten geese swoops down from the back of the cove, honking their way across the bay. They pass over us, almost within grabbing distance. I hear the heavy beat of their strong wings flapping against the air. The formation passes the Bayliner and veers sharply to the left, down the narrow channel at the edge of Protection Island.

* * * * *

After coffee the next morning, we raise anchor. We head for Refuge Cove, almost directly across the strait from Squirrel Cove. This is traditionally a zoo-like fuel stop in mid-summer, but I expect no problems today. In fact, I'm not certain we'll find the fuel dock open, but we can easily make it to Lund for gas, if necessary.

The weather has held as expected, although the southeast winds are forecast to increase as the day progresses. It's a short trip across the channel. Halfway across, I adjust my aiming point to the right to make landfall close to the entrance to Refuge Cove. It's a well-disguised entry, although obvious once you get closer. I sight the large red marker at Hope Point just as Margy reminds me I'm passing the entrance.

"Do you see the entrance?" she asks.

"Sure. I was about to make the turn," I lie, and she knows I'm faking it. This is an entrance I should not have missed with the big red marker to guide me – red-right-returning. I now need to turn back to the left sharply to keep the marker on my right. We slip into the harbour without further incident.

It's a far cry from the typical summer scene. The fuel dock is nearly empty, with only one powerboat and a long silver dory with a flat bow. The other docks, farther inward, are mostly vacant.

As I pull up to the dock, the silver dory blasts away. I slide in next to one of the three pumps marked "Gasoline," and Margy hops off the aft deck and efficiently ties up our lines.

On the small hill at the edge of the cove, the cafe displays a large "Closed" sign. I guess breakfast is out of the question. I walk around the corner of the fuel shed. The door to the fueling office is wide open, but no one is inside.

"I think he just went out to the garbage barge," says the powerboat captain, who sits on his rear deck. "I just got my fuel. Then he left."

"Must've seen me coming," I kid. "No problem. I can wait."

I turn to watch the dory pulling up to the garbage barge at the island a kilometre away. While I wait for the dory to return, Margy goes to the general store to see what books are currently on their always-interesting rack. She returns 15 minutes later with a message.

"The store clerk says just pump your own and tell him how many litres you take."

Good enough for me.

Margy volunteers to return to the store with the litre total and pay the bill, so I untie all the lines and loop the stern rope through the wood dock rail. I stand on the dock and hold tension on the line, holding the Bayliner in position until Margy returns. I hand her the rope, and climb the stairs to the command bridge to start the engine. We have an unflappable policy of never releasing the final rope until the engine is running, just in case it doesn't start and we end up floating dead in the water next to the dock.

I'm quick to flip on the blower and start the engine, but the boat starts to drift a bit in the meantime. Margy holds the looped line as tight as she can, but the Bayliner's bow is getting away from her. As soon as she hears the motor start, she tries to step aboard. But she finds herself straddling between dock and boat, as the Bayliner slides away from the dock. I look down at the aft deck just as she's in that all-critical position and yell words of encouragement.

"Am I leaving without you?" I ask sarcastically.

Maybe my encouragement helps, because she immediately gives me a disgusted look, leans into the boat, and thrusts her arm up towards me. From the command bridge, I reach down and grab her hand, and haul her into the boat. She's aboard, just barely, and we're off.

*****

The seas are rough but acceptable. I decide to take the inside route through Thulin Passage to avoid the wave action outside. That requires slowing to pass opposite direction traffic, two sailboats headed north.

Passing Lund, the water gets even rougher in 3-foot swells, but I know it's typical of this stretch. In these southerly winds, conditions should improve as we approach the lee side of Harwood Island.

"It should smooth out soon," I state. "Would you mind stopping to fish near the Atrevida Marker?"

"Sure" is Margy's reply.

The large metal buoy, marking the outside of Atrevida Reef, is a place I've never fished. But a reef is usually a good spot. I plan to drift near the marker as we fish. The hard part is finding the buoy. It's a big anchored float, but usually I'm right on top of it before I see it. Somehow, it blends into the background.

Margy sees the buoy first: "11:30 to 12 o'clock," she says.

I still don't see it, but I steer a bit to the left to close on the position. In a few minutes, I finally see the marker, blending into the background, as usual.

We close on the reef, my plan being to stop just beyond it and drift back. The swells are still pretty exciting, but well under the limits of the boat. The huge buoy is tilting left and right in major oscillations.

I pass the marker and cut the engine about 50 metres beyond. It's time to fish.

The bow swings downwind. Drift in a boat seems different every time, dependent upon the hull design, wind, waves, and a variety of factors I haven't fully mastered. We're rolling from side to side rather significantly, but Margy has her line in the water quickly. It takes me a bit longer to get down from the command bridge and ready to fish. I'm still fumbling with my fishing pole when…

"Wow!" I yell.

Suddenly, seemingly out of nowhere, the Atrevida marker pops into view just off the aft deck. We've blindly and rapidly drifted past it. The huge buoy was blocked by the bow until it suddenly appeared off the stern. I never saw it coming, but it must have missed collision with our boat by only a few metres. At the rate we're drifting, it would've been quite a whack. I grab my camera and snap a photo as the buoy slips farther from the boat. That was too close!

We bob in the swells, casting our lines. Each of us catches a small ling cod. Both fish are below the current legal limit of 26 centimetres,

so they're released. Overhead, the sun bursts through the clouds, an impressive mass of altocumulus that appropriately looks like the scales on a fish: mackerel sky, more wet than dry.

Within another hour, we're back in Westview Harbour and headed for shelter in our condo. The mini-storm moves in fairly rapidly. By sunset, it's raining. Today, the 14th day of June, is a fitting time marker in the cycle of the seasons. In exactly one week, the earth will enter its first official day of summer, and soon thereafter the annual migration of recreational boats will dominate the Strait of Georgia. The parade north is about to begin. But for now, summer is somewhere in the future. We beat the parade.

Chapter 9

Engine Change

Ever on the lookout for used boats and accessories, John is currently in the market for two things I need, at least in his perception of my necessities: a boat trailer and an overhauled engine for the Bayliner. Hiring the local boat shop to move *Halcyon Days* back and forth from Powell Lake to the chuck every year is not only expensive, it's inconvenient. It would be a lot better if we could move the boat on our own schedule, including layovers at the airport for maintenance when coming in and out of the lake. The prospective trailer should be dual axle to handle the 24-foot boat, and such trailers are hard to find on the used market.

The overhauled engine is a lower priority, at least for the time being, since we don't need a new motor yet. But we'll need it eventually – the hours on the current engine are creeping upward – so John is keeping his eyes open. When both an engine and trailer become available in close succession, my wallet can barely stand the joy. But it's hard to pass up a good deal.

Trailering the Bayliner is a rather big haul, even for John, so it would be best if we pulled the Bayliner out the water and relaunched it under controlled conditions. As it turns out, we end up dealing with operation of the new trailer and the engine overhaul (which occurs earlier than expected) nearly simultaneously. It should have been a warning sign, but I don't see it.

* * * * *

A few years ago, if you had asked me whether I ever planned to change a boat engine, I would've laughed. With my mechanical abilities, any consideration of a project on that scale would be considered insurmountable. But under John's supervision, I've gradually undertaken mechanical repairs that prove there's hope for a guy like me from the school of the mechanically declined.

Gradually, after assisting John with tasks in recent years, I've actually begun to develop a mechanical touch. I still have a long way to go, but now I tackle things on my own that I would not have even considered previously. Under John's supervision, I've even assisted in the building of a float cabin (his new Cabin Number 5). That's a lot of progress for someone who has lived his entire life by assigning automobile maintenance, even engine oil changes, to the local car shop.

When the engine on the Bayliner begins to show increasing signs of age, John pushes for a new motor. The engine still runs well most of the time, but it struggles during starts and occasionally flames out when idling. There are a few incidents involving component failures that call my attention to the age of the engine, including the overheating in Okeover Inlet (Chapter 5) and the flameout near Hernando Island (Chapter 7). Maybe most important, the old engine has lost compression. It's a Chevy 305 that quickly brought the boat up on-plane only a few years ago. Now, with a full load of fuel, someone has to be sent to the bow to get the Bayliner up on the step.

There's no doubt this engine will need to be overhauled or replaced in the near future, but it's tough to abandon an engine that's still running fine most of the time. Adding a quart of oil every few hours is a minor inconvenience.

While I'm in the States, John phones to tell me about a bargain he has discovered during his constant scouting for good deals. If it isn't a used boat he's discovered, it might be a good buy on an outboard motor. This time it's an engine for the Bayliner.

"This is the engine you need," says John. "Almost too good to be true."

"So what's the catch?" I ask.

"Well, it's in Sooke, which is a bit of a problem."

John pursues a lot of good deals, then often backs away. You have to chase a lot of bargains to find a real one. Like most of the "for sale" opportunities he finds, this engine is on Vancouver Island, which requires a ferry ride. Sooke is south of Victoria, and just getting there and back would require an overnight stay on the Island.

"Could be a problem with the roads too," I say.

It's February, and Victoria is currently in the news for a partial transportation shutdown because of a recent snowstorm.

"Couldn't make it to Sooke and back in a single day," says John. "But I might be able to cut a deal. I think I can talk the seller into meeting me in Duncan to transfer the engine from their truck to ours."

The engine is an almost-new Chevy 350, a nice upgrade to the Bayliner's current engine. It was removed from a fishing boat in Sooke after only ten hours of operation, and it comes with a full compliment of overhauled accessories.

Since I won't be back in Canada for another week, I give John the go-ahead to cut the deal and buy the engine in my absence. That will take a bit of coordination. How do you transfer a 600-pound engine from one truck to another in Duncan? Can you even make it there and back before the last ferry to Powell River leaves the dock in Comox?

John calls the Canadian Tire store in Duncan, and they agree to provide a forklift to execute the transfer of the engine from one truck to another. He takes the first morning ferry out of Powell River and manages to catch the last ferry home. We have our new engine.

* * * * *

The Bayliner has spent the winter in Powell Lake. Since it's still running relatively well, we plan to continue operating the old engine until something substantial develops. Then we will move *Halcyon Days* to the airport hangar, where we'll do the engine change. In a few months, the Bayliner is destined for the chuck, where we expect to get another season of operation, maybe longer.

Like a finicky kid who's determined to punish his parents, the Bayliner's old engine immediately begins to act up. The motor somehow knows it's destined to be replaced, and decides to punish me. The next time I try to start the engine, it goes into a fit of misfiring. When I finally get it running, it refuses to operate normally. With a revengeful rattle that sounds like the crankshaft is mired in gunk, the motor grinds to a stop. The time has come to change the engine, earlier than I expected.

Of course, the engine might need only minor repairs, but why bother? We have the new engine, and I have a desire to start the summer on the chuck with a new motor. There's no time like the present.

I coordinate a date with John for taking the Bayliner from the cabin to the Shinglemill, then to the airport. That morning, Margy prepares the Campion while I make one more try at starting the Bayliner. Margy will drive in formation with me, in case the temperamental engine makes it only halfway, and the Campion will serve as our transportation back to the cabin.
I have towing ropes standing by to assure we complete the journey.

When I crank the starter, the noise is unlike any I've heard before. The sharp grinding sound is enough to cause me to abort the start.

"Looks like we get to tow the Bayliner all the way," I say to Margy.

"That engine knows it's being replaced," she replies.

I really do believe some machines have a human personality. To be abandoned necessitates revenge, and we're receiving it this morning.

* * * * *

"Hey, John! This is towboat number one, just north of Cassiar Island, headed for the Shinglemill," I say over the cell telephone.

"You're towing it?" he says. "What happened?"

"Wouldn't even start. But it tows fine. Should be at the Shinglemill by about noon."

"You can park at the dock for now, but we won't be able to use the ramp at the Shinglemill," he says. "Water's too low. We'll need to take it out of the lake at Mowat Bay."

This makes things even more complicated. Already, we face multiple trips in trucks and cars to extract the Bayliner from the lake. Now, with the Shinglemill boat ramp too shallow for our new-to-us trailer which is quite low-slung, our crisscross route will take all afternoon.

The low water level has become a problem for a lot of boaters and cabin owners. We're currently within a few inches of the lowest lake level I've ever seen, and it's still dropping. The cement ramp at the Shinglemill is barely in the water, and our boat trailer needs lots of water.

According to John, Mowat Bay isn't much better, but the drop-off at the end of the cement ramp is more acceptable. He's still concerned, but we should be able to extract the Bayliner there. But that's where it gets complicated.

The just-purchased trailer needs to be licensed, so that means a trip to town to get the tags. Then, after hitching up the trailer at the airport, we'll need two vehicles (Margy's truck and my old Ford Tempo) to complete the project. John will head to Mowat Bay with the truck and trailer, while Margy and I go to the Shinglemill in the Tempo to tow the Bayliner to Mowat with the Campion. Then Margy will drive the Campion back to the Shinglemill, while John and I tow the Bayliner to the airport. It's a complicated maze of travel with two boats, two motor vehicles three people, and a dog.

John is waiting for us on the dock at the Shinglemill. He helps tie up our two boats, and then we drive to town to begin our chores. A few hours later, Margy and I are inbound to Mowat Bay, towing the Bayliner behind the Campion. John awaits us, while Bro runs along the shore hunting for beach critters to play with.

John has parked the truck with its rear wheels at the very limit of the cement ramp, which is totally out of the water. The trailer is in the mix of rocks and sand at the water's edge, sitting slightly tilted. When we maneuver the Bayliner onto the trailer and try to winch it forward, it barely moves onto the bunks. But by rocking the boat, we finally get it within a foot of the bow roller.

To make matters even more complex, this is the first time for the Bayliner on this trailer, so we're concerned with proper balance. The trailer's forward winch rack has been set in a position we expect will be adequate. But now we see that two feet of boat overhangs the rear bunks of the trailer. The gas tanks (both main and auxiliary) are nearly empty, promoting a more-forward center of gravity, but John is still concerned.

"Looks okay," says John. "But we'll know more when we start up the ramp."

We secure the safety chain and add an extra rope from boat to trailer, just in case. A hefty John-knot in the rope assures we won't lose the Bayliner on the way back to the airport.

"Shall I climb aboard to see how it feels before we pull it out?" I ask.

"Sure," replies John. "But be careful, in case it rocks."

"Looks precarious to me," says Margy.

I carefully climb aboard. Standing on the rear deck, all feels solid. I rock my weight back and forth, and the Bayliner remains steadfast. While I'm in the boat, I raise the leg and turn off the battery master switch.

John needs four-wheel-drive to pull the boat up the ramp. There's some minor skidding on the concrete, but the toughest part of the journey is now behind us. So we think.

We pause just above the ramp to survey the boat's position on the trailer. It seems firmly on the bunks, though tilted to the starboard a little and sticking out two feet from the rear of the trailer. We pull the drain plug, and head for the airport.

* * * * *

At the airport, John backs the Bayliner into the hangar. We take some time to position the rear of the boat under the overhead beam we intend to use as a winching point for removal of the engine. Then we try to unhook the trailer.

The latch for the hitch ball is jammed. We try relieving the load on the ball by repositioning the trailer's forward jack. Then we jiggle the latch by moving the truck back and forth. Still, the latch remains jammed. We work at it for about fifteen minutes, pushing, pulling, and jiggling.

"We could remove the truck's bumper," I kid.

"Hey, that's not a bad idea," replies John.

I know he's not serious, but I've given him an idea.

"We could disconnect the truck's tow bar and then pull forward," he says. "Then the pressure will be off the latch so we can get it loose."

But why is there pressure on the latch? In John's voice, I can tell he's asking the same question. Trailer latches have a built-in safety mechanism to prevent connecting or disconnecting them if there's improper loading on the latch. We both understand the safety mechanism, and we are about to bypass it's intent.

It's a case of mutual leap before you look, which may be like me, but it's not like John. Yet we proceed with the plan without any further hesitation. John hops aboard the truck, while I remain back at the trailer to watch the truck slowly pull the tow bar housing off the hitch bar. The truck moves only a few inches forward, and the bar comes loose.

"Oh, my!" I yell, as the trailer tips backwards.

The front of the trailer thrusts itself well above my head, but I don't hear any crunching sounds from the rear. Maybe we've dodged a very big bullet.

"Holy crap!" shouts John as he quickly exits the truck, and runs back to join me.

"So that's why the latch wouldn't come off," I say. "There was too much weight on the rear of the trailer."

"Obviously!" exclaims John.

The trailer sits tilted precariously downward at the rear. We've lucked out. The plunging rear end has stopped just short of the ground. The stern drive skeg sits a mere inch from the hangar floor.

Using our full body weight, we're able to pull the front of the trailer down. Margy and I sit on the tow bar while John places jacks under the rear. Then he proceeds to stabilize the boat with another jack under the center.

All is okay for now, but we'll need to pull the boat forward on the trailer for increased stability. During its stay in the hangar, we'll need to hook up the truck and adjust the trailer several times as we go through the engine removal and replacement. The current center of gravity simply won't do. So we spend some time moving the winch rack forward, preparing for a trip back to the lake to refloat the boat and readjust it's position on the trailer.

We remove the dinghy (about 100 pounds) to alleviate some of the aft weight. Then we hook up to the truck again, and head back to Mowat Bay. With the lake level so low, we're barely able to get the trailer in deep enough to allow the boat to float. But we maneuver the boat off the trailer, then back on. With precise positioning of the truck and trailer, we manage to get enough buoyancy (when I stand on the rear swim-grid) to pull the boat forward an additional two feet. It's a better fit, but it's tough to keep the boat level as we pull it out of the water. On the first try, when we stop to inspect the situation, John isn't satisfied.

"Not good enough," he says. "The balance is fine now, and I'm sure we've got enough weight on the tow bar. But look at how tilted it is."

"Tilted to the right," I say. "But it's tough getting it level with the low water level. Hey, it's only tilted a little."

Tilted a little is not good enough for John.

"Let's try it again," says John. "This time you stay aboard and shift your weight to settle the boat onto the trailer more evenly."

So we return to Mowat Bay, and try again. But John is still not satisfied. Bro sits on the launch ramp, watching us go back and forth, in and out of the lake, seeking the perfection that John demands. It takes three tries before he accepts the boat's position as adequate.

* * * * *

Once the boat is securely in the hangar (no jacks required), removal of the engine proceeds smoothly. In only a few hours, we have the stern drive removed in preparation for disconnection of the motor.

Several hours are needed to remove all of the engine wiring, the engine mounts, and the connections it to the stern leg.

We install a chain block to the overhead beam, and the old engine is raised out of the boat. There are few problems, since it's a tight fit. Removal of the water pump on the front of the engine provides

just enough clearance to move the engine forward and upward. Then the boat and trailer are pulled forward, to allow the old engine to be dropped down onto a small quad trailer.

Then the process is reversed to hoist the new Chevy 350 into position. We're now almost ready to lift the motor into the boat.

John selects some accessories from the old engine that are better than those on the new engine (e.g., the old starter is a better design than the new one), and he proceeds to install them. Meanwhile, I'm in charge of cleaning out the bilge in preparation for the new engine. One of my tasks is to drain both fuel tanks to check for contamination. I've always suspected that the auxiliary tank contains contaminants that caused the old engine to run rough (or stop altogether) when the fuel quantity got low. This will be a good time to purge the tanks of any water or contaminants.

I attack the main tank first, unbolting the fuel quantity sender unit to gain access to the metal tank. When I siphon out the two gallons of fuel remaining in the tank, the bright pink liquid looks clear. I add another gallon of gas to the tank and siphon it with similar results. The liquid is so clear that I'm tempted to reuse it, but I don't.

The aux tank contains 5 gallons of fuel, so it's a slower process. At first the gas is clear and brilliant pink, like the main tank. Then

the fluid running through my siphon hose becomes suddenly milky white. In fact, there's barely a hint of pink in the liquid as it pours out into my pail. After filling the container, I stop momentarily before continuing.

"Take a look at this!" I yell to John, who is down on the hangar floor, working on the new engine that sits on a pallet.

I lift the container over the transom and set it down on the swim-grid so John can see it. The milky white fluid has settled to the bottom, distinctly separated from the bright pink gas. A significant amount of water has become entrapped in the fuel. When the aux tank runs low on fuel, the motor has been trying to burn almost pure water.

The aux tank's fuel cap is mounted horizontally on the aft deck, in a position where it receives the direct assault of rain. When we look close, we find a small hole in the top of the cap that may have originally been a vent line. We seal the hole, and also replace the fuel filter. With the aux tank drained and refilled with gas, our tanks should be good-to-go for many more years.

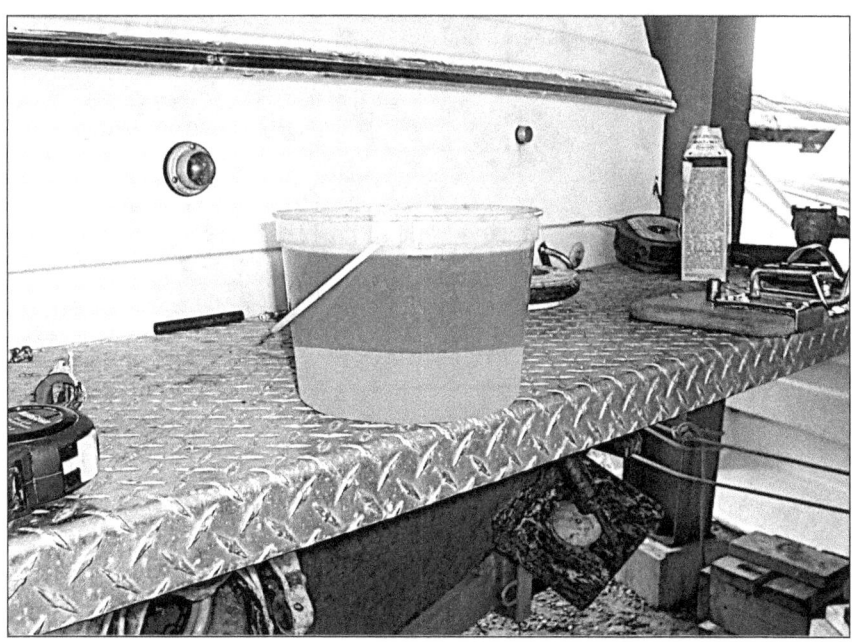

* * * * *

When we finally hoist the new engine into the boat, I consider it a momentous occasion. I've already learned more about boat engines than I ever expected to glean. Working with John is always that way.

The tight confines of the engine compartment require dropping the new engine down at an angle. John adds a strap to the chain block that keeps the front of the engine higher than the rear. This allows the drive shaft to slip in first, thus making room for the front of the engine (with the water pump removed for additional clearance).

John's dad, Ed, arrives just in time to assist with the installation. He's the top wizard in a family of mechanically-inclined sons. When the going gets tough, Ed usually shows up to provide valuable hints to his boys.

Slowly, the motor is lowered the rest of the way into the engine compartment, clearing the main fuel tank by less than an inch. Once it's safely inside, John eases the engine onto new mounting plates he has built.

Rewiring the new engine becomes a challenge. We're converting from old-fashioned mechanical distributor points to an electronic ignition system. Matching up the wiring in the old boat to this task is a process that causes John considerable work, including lots of soldering and tracing out wiring diagrams.

When we run into difficulties matching up the wires, Ed comes to the rescue. He finds what he needs on the Internet, but his printer won't print out the wiring diagram properly. Foregoing the simplest (but not least-costly solution) of purchasing the diagrams on-line, Ed sits before the computer monitor and copies by hand the wiring schematics. His final product may not be repair manual format, but it gives us what we need to wire up the engine.

"I don't see where this white wire goes," says John. "I'll just tape it off – probably not important."

"Better not," replies Ed. "You might fry everything."

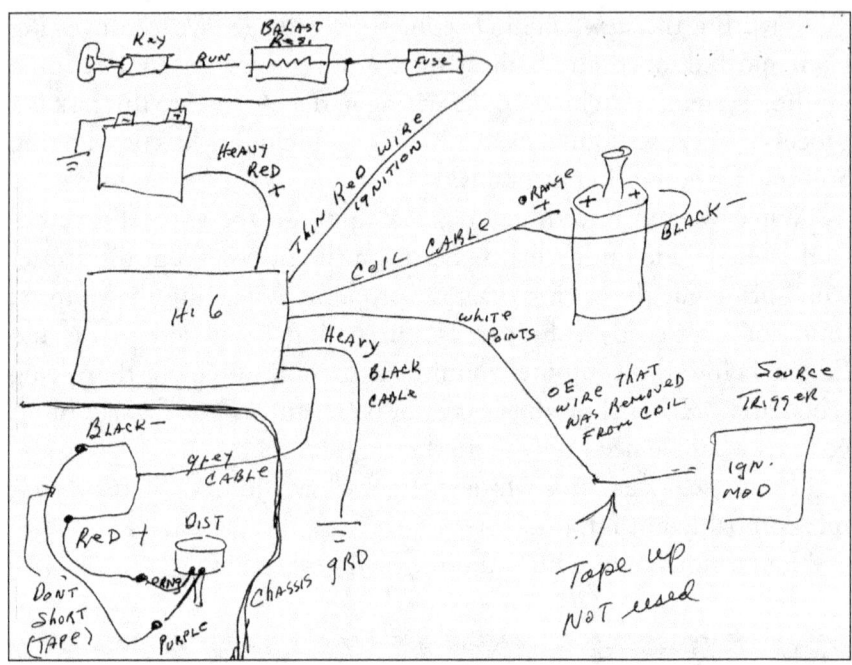

It's often difficult to know when Ed is kidding. But I notice that John changes his mind and traces out the white wire on the schematic.

In a few hours, all wires are identified and connected. Then we turn our attention to the stern leg. Mounting it involves the connection of several hoses that are difficult to get at, and some of the bolts are designed for shops with special tools. So John designs his own tools as he goes along.

"Hand me that socket extension," he says, pointing to the tools lying on the swim-grid. "It'll slip in there, by that exhaust hose, and we can use it to rotate the hose clamp."

Nearly ready for our first engine run, we hook up the "cuffs" that provides cooling water from a garden hose. We'll be able to run the engine right here in the hangar with the prop not yet installed. If it starts, that is.

We still have some final details to attend to on the engine, but the day is drawing to a close, and John wants to try starting it.

"We'll just see if there's a spark," says John.

He removes a spark plug, grounds it to the engine, and holds it with his foot to insulate himself from the jolt. Then he assigns me to the helm to make the first crank of the new engine.

The engine rotates normally, with all of the expected starting sounds. But there is no spark.

As if on cue, John's brother, Rick, shows up in the hangar. Probably Ed has told him about our battle with the wiring diagram, and he has stopped by to see how we're doing.

"No spark," says John disgustedly.

"Let's look over the wiring one more time," says Rick.

Together, the two brothers scratch their heads over the electronic ignition system, tracing out each wire in sequence. Rick seems to know even more about engines than John, although it's a close call.

By the time we leave the hangar at 6 o'clock, we still don't have ignition.

* * * * *

The next day, looking for a diversion to this wiring nightmare, we tackle some of the simpler projects that still remain. Both VHF antennas need to be replaced, victims of a strange accident at the cabin. The two fragile plastic antennas were attacked simultaneously by a large flying plastic table top. The collision occurred when I was in the States. While Margy rode out a major storm at the cabin, a strong wind tossed the heavy plastic tabletop off the cabin deck right at the docked Bayliner. The results could've been worse (except for the price of the new antennas). The replacement process goes smoothly.

Next on our list is one of my most anticipated projects – installation of a new moving-map GPS on the command bridge. I have plenty of portable GPS receivers for a variety of uses, but this new model has a bigger screen with elaborate new features. It incorporates a depth sounder that will replace the Bayliner's old-style analogue receiver which works only when it's in the mood (and that's not often). The new depth sounder incorporates a fish-finder that displays cute little fish symbols just itching to be caught.

Call it unnecessary extravagance, if you like, but I look forward to these improvements. John calls it pure overkill. He's particularly animated in his attitude when he finds out how much the new GPS costs. A boater like John enjoys navigating by reference to landmarks, so satellite navigation isn't necessarily a step forward. And he's never met a depth sounder that worked properly.

"Do you really need GPS," he laments. "Can't you just find out where you are with a chart? And those fish-finders are notoriously inaccurate when they display those fish symbols swimming below the boat?"

There's no real answer that will suffice, so I try not to fight it. Maybe when he sees the new equipment in action, he'll feel better.

We mount the transducer for the depth sounder on the transom, positioned precisely as shown in the installation instructions. In the process, an old wiring bundle to the command bridge has to be upgraded with new wire and connectors. Within a few hours the complete system is installed and ready for initial power-up.

When we turn on the receiver, the warm-up screen appears in vivid colours. John hits the "Map" button, and a brilliant regional chart appears, with the warning: "Satellites looking for position." It's unlikely the GPS will find any satellites under this metal hangar roof, but the display is bright and impressive. Even John exhales a respectful "Oh!"

Not only are the satellites unavailable here, we're also raised above the hangar floor by 4 feet, with no water between us and the ground, so I don't expect an accurate depth sounding. Without the usual medium (water), I'm looking for the sounder to be only in the ballpark. The reading pops into view almost immediately: "9.5 feet".

"See, I told you it's crap," says John, with a sense of satisfaction.

I switch to the seafloor map view, which shows images of the "ocean" floor passing below, including lots of pretty colours and moving lines. Then three big fish start slowly swimming across the screen. They wiggle realistically as they move.

John starts laughing and simply can't stop.

"Man, that fish-finder is terrific!" he exclaims. "Must be mosquitoes flying under the boat."

Or maybe it's hangar salmon.

* * * * *

The next morning, when I turn on the cell telephone at the cabin, there's a message waiting for me from 9 o'clock the night before. It's the happy voice of John.

"It's running!" he announces proudly. "Found the problem in the manual, and went back out to the airport tonight and fixed it. She runs!"

By noon, we're back in the hangar and finishing up the details. We're getting ready to haul the boat for it's first sea trial. The "sea" will be Powell Lake, a more docile environment if we run into problems. When the new engine is pronounced properly healthy, we'll move the Bayliner to the chuck.

At Mowat Bay, the lake is even lower than when we brought the boat down from the cabin, so we struggle with getting the trailer in position. But then we're floating, a memorable occasion.

The first sea (lake) trial is brief. The engine starts and runs fine, but the voltmeters (both on the command bridge and in the downstairs cabin) read only 10.5 volts, and the oil pressure gauge is pegged off-scale low. We don't get beyond half-throttle before John decides to take the boat back to the dock, then out of the water again. Still, in its brief period in the lake, the boat accelerates nicely and gets nearly on-plane. But the low voltage means the alternator isn't charging the battery, an unacceptable circumstance. And the oil pressure gauge should be fixed right away.

Getting the boat out of the water once again requires our close attention, since the truck's rear wheels are beyond the limit of the concrete ramp. But we pull the Bayliner out without any significant problems. Then we head back towards the hangar. But it would be nice to take the boat to John's house instead. Our repairs should be simple, or so we hope, and it would be nice to have Ed's expertise right there at home to help us troubleshoot these problems.

So rather than drive to the airport, we head for John's house. We back the boat into the vehicle overflow area near the car porch, normally clogged by Rick's two taxi cabs and his truck, John's truck, and an occasional stray quad trailer.

Ed and John pull out the maintenance manual and peruse the wiring diagrams. It seems apparent that the alternator isn't putting out the proper voltage, but first they work together to verify the situation with a multimeter.

John calls Dan at the boat shop to discuss what he's found. Dan listens patiently, but there's little more that can be done relative to the alternator until it's thoroughly tested.

We remove the alternator and take it to the local electrical motor shop, where rows of overhauled starters and alternators are displayed on wide shelves. The friendly proprietor gives us his immediate attention, drops what he's doing, and puts the alternator on his test stand, where he declares it fully healthy.

"Must be the ground connection," he says. "Let me clean that up for you. No charge."

We leave the shop knowing the alternator is serviceable, now with a better ground. Back at the boat, John reinstalls the alternator. Then we hook up the cuffs to the stern drive and turn on the garden hose. I start the engine, and John checks the alternator output – still only 10.5 volts.

Ed and John pour over the wiring diagrams again. John checks some connections suggested by Ed. Finally, we find the culprit – the master fuse that ties the battery into the electrical system.

We buy a new fuse at the boat shop, and make a brief engine run to verify all is well. The alternator problem is solved, but the oil pressure gauge remains inoperative.

Ed climbs up onto the command bridge and checks the instrument panel while John rewires the connections to the oil pressure transmitter. In just a few minutes, that problem is also solved.

Now it's back to Mowat Bay for another sea trial. This time, with the alternator and oil pressure working, we're able to bring the boat up to full speed. Does it ever go!

The new engine is smoother and significantly more powerful, getting up on-plane quickly. John is all smiles. As for me, I'm thrilled with the results, and I can't wait to drive the boat back to the cabin, where I'll continue breaking in the new engine for the next few days.

Back at the dock, I help John bring the tools to shore that he has brought along for the sea trials. In just a few minutes, I'm back in the boat, up on the command bridge, and headed home to Hole in the Wall. The skies have darkened, and the waves are spouting a few white caps. But I'm comfortably on-plane with a sturdy boat and a new engine.

That evening, I'm home with my boat and its new engine, ready to spend a few weeks exploring the lake in the Bayliner. As spring eases into summer, I'll have the chance to assure the engine is ready for the more-challenging chuck. By the beginning of summer, we'll be headed for Desolation Sound and the majestic inlets to the north.

◊ ◊ ◊ ◊ ◊ ◊

Chapter 10

Gorge Harbour

The year after Ken and Sam cruise to Alaska with their new 28-foot Eaglecraft, they plan a shorter trip with the Gibsons Yacht Club. Although the club's annual trip is on schedule, the weather isn't, with cool rain and wind lasting for several days in mid-June. I've already decided not to go north to the Broughtons with them, but I want to meet Ken and Sam when they catch up with the slower sailboats and trawlers. They plan to leave late and still beat the others, and Margy and I can travel with them in the local waters in our Bayliner.

The yacht club has already moved north from Westview's South Harbour. When Ken and Sam finally leave Gibsons, they stop in Powell River, where we join them for dinner.

"Keep in touch for the next few days," I say to Ken. "We don't want to be away from our cabin very long right now, but we should be able to catch up with you on your way back south. Maybe we can spend a night together in Desolation Sound."

The suggestion that Ken keep in contact is possible due to his extensive electronic presence on any ocean trip. The bright yellow crew boat design of *Mr. Buttercup* includes radio gear crammed everywhere. Ken has recently added a second Raymarine moving map to form duplicate consoles up front, and his boat is full of communication equipment. Besides VHF, he's set up to deal with the Internet at every port that can accommodate him. And he's a major presence on the ham boater's network. Mr. Buttercup is a maze of antennas, cables, and connectors for every occasion.

I, on the other hand, will be typically out of communication at my float cabin. The cell phone, although equipped with an external antenna, is normally turned off, and there's no Internet. I hope to keep it that way forever.

"I'll call when we get back down in this area," says Ken. "But you'll need to turn your phone on once in a while."

"For you, I'll do it," I reply. "Every morning and each evening, until I hear from you."

During the next week, when I'm in town, there are several email messages waiting for me from ports to the north, including Port McNeil. *Mr. Buttercup* is now headed south.

"We're in Refuge Cove, home of great Internet. Not like Powell River, which was the only place on the whole trip without it!"

Ken's right – Powell River's transient boating facilities are very limited. If it weren't for the innovative 'We'll raft you up somewhere' attitude of Jim, the wharfinger, there would be no space for visitors in the summer.

In Toba Inlet, Ken finds a pleasant surprise: "We're at Toba Wildernest Resort. No shore power, but they have Internet! We're running on batteries, so hope we still have power in the morning. Cell phone doesn't work here. Not sure where we'll be tomorrow, but will try to get an email out in the morning."

Since I'm about to shut down my computer and depart back up the lake, I type out a reply before I go: "Email won't get to me after 'right now.' We're headed back up the lake, with no Internet. I'll leave my cell phone on continually now until I hear from you. Once you're back in telephone territory, (Sunday, Monday, or whenever), let us know where you're headed next, and Margy and I'll be on our way to find you. It'll take us only about three hours after talking to you to make it back down the lake, load the Bayliner, and be on our way."

Three hours is a rather optimistic estimate, since this will be our first voyage on the chuck this year. Although the boat is basically loaded, getting ready for the first trip always seems to take longer than expected. And we'll need to stop at the condo first. But Margy and I are intent on meeting Ken and Sam, so we're prepared to get going fast when we get the telephone call.

* * * * *

The next day, my telephone rings at 2:05 pm, and I answer it with a challenge for Ken.

"Tell me about Dutch Disease," I state, before Ken can even tell me where he is.

"Don't remember all the details," says Ken. "But I know it killed the guilder."

Ken is a retired professor of economics from UBC, and I'm an enthusiastic amateur economist. Or so I imagine myself. Dutch Disease has been in the news lately as an economic parallel to the escalating Canadian loonie and the current glut of oil exports. In the Netherlands in the 1970s, a similar situation with natural gas and the Dutch currency was enough to kill the economy in almost all areas except the gas industry. I, of course, need to know if Ken thinks it could happen in Canada.

"But you can tell me about it later today," I say. "Where should I meet you?"

"We're in Gorge Harbour on Cortes Island. Lots of dock space. How soon can you get going?"

"Right now. Check that – I should hang up the phone first."

Ken laughs, and asks me for an estimate of what time I think we'll leave Powell River.

"I promised three hours, and that should work. So we should be out of the harbour by five o'clock."

"I'll try calling again at five to check your progress," promises Ken.

"If there's no answer, that means we're ahead of schedule and already out of cell coverage."

It's pretty optimist.

* * * * *

Back in town, we pull up in front of the condo at 3:10 pm, pretty much a record for us. The boat trip down the lake consumes almost a half-hour. Getting ready to leave the cabin, without knowing how long we'll be gone, takes some preparation. An hour door-to-door isn't bad.

I maintain a bag I always take to the Bayliner. It sits in a corner of the condo with stuff I've accumulated for a trip on the chuck since our last outing. Packing is simple, but I take advantage of our location to take a quick shower. I find Margy in the living room, starting up her computer.

"Don't you dare!" I chastise her.

She knows what I'm referring to. It isn't the computer – it's the Internet. When either of us tries to quickly deal with the net, it's a lost cause.

"You're right," she replies, giving in without an appeal.

As soon as her computer finishes starting up, she shuts it down. We're out of the door by 3:35, another record in a series of actions that really don't seem very rushed. We're fast, we're efficient, and we're headed for the chuck.

* * * * *

When I step down from the aft deck into the Bayliner's cabin, I'm greeted by a gift from John and his brother, Rick. They used the boat last, and it should be no surprise that they've left me a present. In this case, it's a two-foot-diameter mooring ball, dark gray in colour and covered with dried seaweed and encrusted white worms. It'll look great floating at the cabin, but for now it will have to go along for the ride to Gorge Harbour. I pick it up and place it in the captain's chair, hooking a bungie around its plastic handle. Since we'll be on the command bridge for the trip, the big ball will be the captain. (Later, at the cabin, I paint the mooring ball half-and-half red and white. It floats loosely attached by a rope to the breakwater boom, and I call it the "Big Bobber," a name appreciated only by those who remember the similarly named singer of the 1950's.)

As we get the Bayliner ready to go, Margy and I attend to our normal tasks. She services the water tank with the dockside hose and unties the dock lines and straps them to their respective rails on the boat. Meanwhile, I remove the canvas cover from the command bridge, setup the GPS, and inspect the engine compartment.

I check my watch as we push off the dock – 3:55. We're a full hour ahead of schedule, only two hours from cabin to chuck!

No sooner are we out in the marina's main channel than I have to shift into reverse and retreat back towards our dock finger. Coming directly towards us is a large sailboat, barely moving, with its main sail fluttering in the nearly calm conditions. The boat is tacking from side to side, so our path is blocked.

A small powerboat is following the sailboat, and we'll need to let them both pass before we can proceed. I back the Bayliner farther into the open area between our dock and the adjacent finger, where I can shift into idle and drift for a few minutes. As the sailboat finally passes, I ease out into the channel. The sailboat captain waves to me and explains.

"Comin' in without an engine," he says. "Pretty slow with barely a wind."

"Hey, I'd like to stick around to see you dock," I kid.

"It might not be pretty," he replies.

Once outside the rock breakwater of the North Harbour, the Bayliner enters a sea that's nearly flat. On this hot afternoon in late June, altocumulus clouds are moving in, providing an overhead crackled pavement look – another maceral sky, more wet than dry.

The temperature has already hit 28 C, but the clouds should make the rest of the day comfortable. Conditions are perfect, but our fuel is minimal. So we head north to Lund for gas. When starting out on any trip to the north, it always seems more efficient to make an en route stop for fuel rather than motor around to the South Harbour where the gas dock is located.

Lund is a surprise – no boats at the gas dock on a perfect summer Sunday, only two days before Canada Day. I expect the dock to be bustling with activity, but instead, I need to ring the bell for a fuel attendant. Gasoline has pushed over $1.40 per litre this year, and there appears to be no end in sight. With the Canadian dollar stronger than ever, and gas prices still rising, American tourists are forecast to be a rare visitor this summer. The impact on our marine economy may be devastating.

As I pump gas into the main and then the auxiliary tank, several boats enter the harbour. One is a Savary Island water taxi, not a big boat, but enough to set the dock into motion. Another even-smaller boat passes close by at moderate speed, and the fuel dock begins to oscillate. I've never seen a dock more susceptible to swells, probably due to the confined geography of the harbour rather than the dock's structure. Once, after pumping fuel here, I climbed up onto the command bridge to make a cell phone call and nearly became seasick. The simplest solution that day was to simply shove off from the dock and get back into the much calmer ocean.

Fortunately, it's not quite as rough at the dock today. Just as I finish filling the tanks, even before I can put the gas caps back on, the phone rings. It's precisely 5 o'clock, so there's no doubt who's calling.

"Lund here! We're on our way."

I hear a round of rough static, occasionally interspersed with a few broken words from Ken. I try again.

"Ken, if you hear me, you're breaking up badly. We're in Lund, just finishing up with fuel. See you in about an hour and a half."

More static, another spurt of unrelated words from Ken, and then silence. He has hung up.

* * * * *

The trip conditions from here are as perfect as it gets. From Lund, we head out and around the Copeland Islands, then west through Baker Passage that divides Hernando Island from Cortes. It's necessary to skirt the southern tip of Cortes with a wide turn. Rocks can be seen jutting far out to sea from the island, and the shallow shoals we can't see are of even more concern.

Once we sight the buoy marking the outermost extent of the submerged bank of rocks, it becomes a comfortable aiming point. We round the marker and can now head directly for Gorge Harbour. But even when we get close, the narrow entrance is still hidden. Then, suddenly, it opens up to reveal its canyon-like walls.

We slow to below-plane speed and ride into the towering ravine, hugging the north cliffs. I steer the Bayliner away from the big rock at the inside end of the gorge, reduce to no-wake speed, and we slip into the harbour.

Once inside, the harbour has the feeling of a sanctuary, cut off from the powerful ocean by the narrow entrance. A few boats are anchored between us and the marina, so I follow a zigzag path to keep well clear of them.

"There's Sam!" says Margy, pointing to the south end of the docks.

There's little doubt that it's Sam. Her small, thin structure is less of a giveaway than her boisterous waving of arms, a sure sign it's the always enthusiastic Sam. When we get closer, she uses both arms to point to the entry point to our right, and then redirects her motion down a finger where the prominent yellow *Mr. Buttercup* is parked.

Since she has pointed distinctly to our right, I make an immediate maneuver to the left. Sam stops, looks at me intently, and props her hands on her hips in mock disgust. I immediately turn back to the right. Never argue with Sam, but its fun to try.

As I turn down the row of docks, I can see the space between *Mr. Buttercup* and a bigger powerboat as my obvious assigned spot. To get into it and remain facing the same direction as everyone else, I'll need to turn around. There's plenty of room to do that, but it takes a few forward-reverse shifts to complete the turn. On each shift of gears, we drift closer to *Mr. Buttercup*, though I feel well in control of the situation. At this point, Sam is shouting instructions as well as waving her arms. She's never seen me drive a boat before, and she's read too many of my books. I can see the look of concern on her face, particularly since the Bayliner's stern will be passing close to *Mr. Buttercup's* bow during the swing.

My last shift into forward is accompanied by the final turn to set the drift past the yellow bow. I'll clear it nicely (but close enough to suggest mastery of docking), and now I'll only need to shift into reverse one final time to kiss up against the dock. I swing the wheel to the right to allow me to kick the ass around in reverse, and I slap the shift lever into reverse – but it's the throttle instead! *Vroom* goes the engine as it revs up, catching everyone's attention. I immediately come back on the throttle and shift into reverse. The crisis is averted, but Sam's face is the first one I see when I look towards the dock. She gives me a stare that suggests I've done this on purpose just to stir her up.

In reality, I've made this costly mistake several times before. On this boat, the throttle and shift lever are separate, unlike the Campion I drive more regularly. The best solution to avoid this is to keep your hand on the shift lever during the entire docking maneuver, so it can't slip to the throttle by mistake. Seldom is the throttle lever needed once the engine has been set in idle for docking. But today I get the two levers confused in front of everyone at a critical moment. It's a good thing I'm used to embarrassment at sea.

Once everything settles down, we set our docking lines and have a good laugh (at me, and with me). I try to change the subject.

"So I'm waiting for the details about Dutch Disease," I say to Ken.

Not surprisingly, he responds with a thorough explanation of the financial situation in the Netherlands during the 1970s. He doesn't think it's similar to the current economic conditions in Canada.

"If enough economists make a prediction, one of them is sure to be right," he says. "That doesn't mean any of them know what's going on. I'd say our situation is completely different now, but who am I to say?"

That's Ken – always knowledgeable, modest, and fun to listen to. More often than not, his economic predictions are pretty accurate. And his easy-going nature always makes me enthusiastically soak it all in. We walk along the steeply inclined sidewalk near shore, talking about economics.

* * * * *

The next morning, when I step out of the Bayliner, Ken is already engaged in conversation with a middle-age bearded fellow near the end of the dock. The man, short in stature and dressed in black shirt and shorts, is sitting in an inflatable dinghy, showing Ken something.

"Look what this fellow's got," says Ken, waving me over.

The man sits next to a plastic box with what looks like a plumbing pipe sticking out of it at an angle. On the seat next to him is a yellow-and-blue device that looks like a model airplane.

"Hi, I'm Joe," says the man, reaching out to shake my hand. "I hear you might be interested in an underwater camera."

As a matter of fact, I am. Ken and I have been discussing the purchase of an underwater camera for several months. At one point, Ken almost bought a "Fish TV" system for both of us when he was in Oregon, but decided it was more of a toy than a practical instrument. Since then, we've been comparing notes, trying to find an underwater camera that's both inexpensive and semi-professional. Ken wants one for his boat, to inspect the hull, transducers, and such. For me, the thrill of the concept is marine life, but I'd also like to see what lies under my float cabin.

Joe is a marine biologist who taught at the famous Scripts Institute of Oceanography in San Diego before taking an early retirement. Now he spends a lot of his time in coastal BC, exploring for marine life. This morning, he's using his "kick-around" underwater camera to check along the docks for salt water critters. Through an amazing coincidence, one of his current passions is the design of underwater cameras.

"I do some work for *National Geographic*," says Joe. "Just sold them a rotating camera that sits on the sea floor and studies marine life. I could construct a camera like that for you, if you like."

"What about this model?" I say, pointing to the sleek airplane-like "glider" he's been pulling across the bottom this morning.

"Sure, I could make one of those for you, too, but the rotating camera is a lot more for the money."

Yes, it's about money. But it's also about simplicity. This blue-and-yellow plastic glider uses a waterproof camera and a small colour monitor that's viewed through the plastic pipe to cut down on interference in bright sunlight. It's the perfect design for both Ken and me.

"I could provide you with the basic components, and you could set up your own system," offers Joe. "Would be a lot cheaper. Ken tells me you're a retired aeronautics professor, so you could design it the way you want."

"I'm afraid it's a different brand of aeronautics than you've been led to believe," I reply. "Aeronautics means flying in this case. I'm far from an engineer."

"Oh," says Joe. "I see what you mean. Well, I can do whatever you want, but you could get a lot of the parts yourself. I use this DVD player to record what I see and add my own comments through a microphone. You could do the same."

I convince Joe that anything mechanical (or electronic) would probably be over my head, so he agrees to construct a complete system for me. Ken, on the other hand, will probably opt to do much of the system setup himself.

"I'm not very interested in the wildlife," says Ken. "I'll use it mostly for checking out things on my boat."

At first it sounds insulting to me. Telling a marine biologist you aren't interested in "wildlife" seems similar to telling an astronomer you're not interested in the sky. But Joe just nods his head in understanding.

"Actually, you'd be amazed how much other stuff you'll find down there," he says. "Barbecues and all kinds of things."

I picture a marine biologist of *National Geographic* calibre poking around looking at discarded pieces of underwater junk.

"But the marine life must be the real thrill for you," I say.

"Amazing stuff," says Joe. "I've got a miniature camera I'm working on now that's almost ready to go. I plan to attach it to the back of a crab with a piece of Velcro and see things from the crab's point of view. Should be fun."

An underwater crab cam. Yes, it would be unique.

I tell Joe about my use of a Kemmerer bottle in Powell Lake, and ask about the powdery precipitate I discovered (*Up the Strait*, Chapters 8 and 13):

"My amateur theory – I have a very active imagination, Joe – involves the fact that the lake water from eleven hundred feet down hasn't seen oxygen for thousands of years. When brought it to the surface, the water reacted with the oxygen in the air. Do you think it might have contained hydrogen sulfide, which is a gas, and then mixed with the free oxygen to form hydrogen sulfate, a precipitate?"

I feel like I'm stumbling – an amateur talking to a professional marine biologist.

"Well, that's not so far fetched," says Joe. "But maybe it's something simpler involving the diatoms in the water. They're everywhere in the

water, and they fall like snow flakes to the bottom. When you turn on a light underwater, those flakes reflect like crazy everywhere. There'd be a lot of diatoms on the floor of the lake, and you might have been seeing them settle out of your sample."

"Makes sense," I reply. "Maybe I could just look at them under my microscope."

"Sure. They're pretty distinctive in shape, so you should be able to tell right away when you magnify the precipitate."

Another great project for a long winter evening in the cabin. And once I get my underwater camera, I'll be even more dangerous.

* * * * *

From Gorge Harbour, we'll travel together, *Halcyon Days* and *Mr. Buttercup*, to Manson's Landing and then to Cortes Bay. Ken hasn't been to either harbour and wants to see them. From there, we plan to circle around the east side of Cortes Island for lunch at Squirrel Cove. Then Ken and Sam will head home for Gibsons, in time for Gibsons'

Canada Day sail-past. All of the club's members are now headed home from their voyage north, and Ken and Sam want to join them for this event.

Margy and I will have a more relaxed schedule, since the trip back to Powell River will be a short one. Then we'll travel up the lake to our float cabin before dark. It has been less than twenty-four hours since we left Powell Lake, and we'll be home after only one night away from the cabin. For us, that's perfect planning.

"Do you want to lead?" I ask Ken. "It really doesn't matter to me whether I follow you or go first."

"I should consult the Skipper," says Ken. "But my guess is she'll prefer you go first."

He refers to Sam with his normal sense of respect and lightness. The Skipper usually has a strong opinion on such matters, and Ken is typically happy with any decision. Sam is a precise thinker, and Ken is a fellow who finds "good enough" to be a comfortable attitude. It works well for them as the Skipper and the Navigator of *Mr. Buttercup*.

We gather up our gear in our respective boats and start our engines. When Ken waves to me, I ask Margy to remove our dock lines, and we're off.

I lead the way out of Gorge Harbour, weaving behind a large powerboat that's temporarily paused in the middle of the bay. A man is scurrying around the aft deck, stowing the dinghy, while a woman on the command bridge tends to the helm. Once I'm clear of this boat, I look behind me to see the powerboat has started out of the harbour behind us, leaving *Mr. Buttercup* in third position.

I travel slow, barely above idle, in respect to the no-wake restrictions. Behind me the two boats follow in precise formation. Once in the gorge, there will be no opportunity to pass, since it's nearly low tide.

Once outside the entrance, I accelerate to on-plane, and the powerboat behind me powers up and veers off to the north toward Uganda Passage. *Mr. Buttercup* can outpace me, and quickly catches up, riding directly behind the Bayliner in the clear area of our wake.

Manson's Landing is crowded, a good sign for summer economics. A variety of boats are anchored along the shore leading to the harbour. In the distance, just past the docks, a large sailboat is tilted precariously

to the side, grounded at low tide. It looks like an embarrassing and potentially expensive incident, but the boat should float again within a few hours.

At the docks, I shift into neutral and hover near the mass of rafted-up boats that make the small marina as full as it can get. A Cessna Caravan on floats pushes away from the dock, leaving a brief open spot. The floatplane starts its turboprop engine and begins to taxi.

Mr. Buttercup pulls up next to us, and Ken and I talk over VHF Channel 69. We'll need to wait for the floatplane to depart.

"Who has the right of way in a case like this?" asks Ken. "Airplane or boat?"

"Since that airplane costs over a million, I'd say he goes first," I reply.

The Caravan roars out of the harbour, away from us, and into the air. I watch the plane climb out of ground effect, level off to accelerate further, and then begin to climb again. Framed by the backdrop of the snow-capped peaks of Vancouver Island to the west, the seaplane continues upward and away. In a few more seconds the roar of its powerful engine disappears. It's time for us to leave.

Once again, I lead us out and around the buoy marking the outer extent of the rocky shoal at the tip of Cortes Island, then back through Baker Passage and into Cortes Bay.

Red-right-returning is a gentle reminder at the entrance to the bay. The opening to the right actually looks larger than the route to the left. But the red marker correctly keeps us on course. I keep it to our right, passing halfway between it and the cliff to our left.

Inside the harbour, only a few boats are anchored, but the government dock has only one empty space. Several spots contain rafted boats.

Only a few hundred metres to the west, the yacht club marina is almost empty. I conclude it's standing ready to receive boats from Vancouver and Seattle in a few days, once the magic July 1st voyage-north date has arrived. Reciprocity agreements between yacht clubs in this region are an efficient way to bring visiting boaters into crowded harbours.

Once again, I shift into neutral and await Ken and Sam. They are just entering the harbour. Meanwhile, Ken and Margy talk over the VHF channel.

"Any open spots?" asks Ken.

"Only one, and it's a small one," replies Margy.

"Looks like lots of space at the Seattle Yacht Club," kids Ken.

"Are you ready to press on to Squirrel Cove?" asks Margy.

There's silence on frequency, while Ken and Sam talk things over. Then Ken responds.

"The Skipper is ready to go home," says Ken, with a sense of satisfaction in his voice.

"No problem," says Margy. "It's been fun. See you soon."

"In Gibsons, maybe," replies Ken.

"Maybe Gibsons," says Margy.

And that's the end of our conversation. There's nothing more to say. The short stay at Gorge Harbour and today's visit to Manson's Landing and Cortes Bay have been a wonderful start to summer.

The Skipper powers up, and we watch the yellow boat disappear out through the harbour entrance. We're all going home.

Chapter 11

Von Donop

My mind is set on Von Donop Inlet on the north end of Cortes Island. Once my mind is set, it's difficult to deviate. To add to this focus, I have an active imagination. And my attention the past few days has been on Von Donop and a fellow named Mark Vonnegut.

The narrow inlet nearly splits Cortes Island, almost connecting to Squirrel Cove on the south side. At one time, the island may have been separated by this waterway. There'll likely be two islands again in the geologic future.

My imagination is under personal scrutiny this evening. I've been in town only a few hours, and it's been a struggle. When I leave my float cabin these days, after a week of solitude, it often turns into a confrontational experience. The clash is with myself, the result of encountering too much humanity too quickly.

This evening, Margy and I move our mobile in-town supplies from her truck to my car. In preparation for her departure for the States in the truck, I'll need some of the truck's equipment, and she prefers an emptier vehicle to ease her border crossing tensions. It's a simple task – moving books, slideshow equipment, boating gear, and other aspects of our mobile life into my Ford Tempo. But tonight I'm overwhelmed by the constant shuffling of stuff (which is our chosen lifestyle), and start yelling at myself. Fortunately, Margy long ago learned to ignore me when I'm in my in-town mood.

In the back of my mind is a book I'm halfway through – *Eden Express* by Mark Vonnegut (Dell Publishing, 1975). If you love the Powell River region for its sublime beauty, this book will leave a lasting impression. Mark settled Fiddlehead Farm on Powell Lake during his hippie days of the early 1970s, and suffered a severe case of schizophrenia along the way. His life on the farm was virtuously satisfying to him, eerily equating to my high-minded introduction to Hole in the Wall. Mark faced significant difficulties during his occasional trips to town. Of course, he was schizophrenic. On the other hand, there's a fine line between sanity and insanity.

This evening, I'm focused on all of the similarities between Mark and me, including his schizophrenic periods with almost no sleep for weeks. I almost always have difficulties trying to sleep at the condo in town. Maybe I shouldn't feel so bad about my adverse reaction to this fine community, and consider it perfectly normal. The comparison settles me, but not until my moving-stuff-rant is over.

A few hours later, with lots of July evening light remaining, I'm at the North Harbour, working with John on swapping the prop on the Bayliner. It's a simple task – simple to John, at least. I watch carefully, making sure I can duplicate the prop removal if I ever need it at sea. I hold the fish net under the raised stern leg as John pulls the prop off the shaft, ready to catch if he errs. It's more symbolic than essential – John will never drop a prop.

We've been fighting the aftermath of the engine change for weeks. First there was the occasional tendency of the engine to continue running when the ignition switch on the command bridge was turned off. Then there was the ingested rope at the Shinglemill when I failed to properly stow a docking line, followed by another bout with the fickle ignition switch. This time, the engine wouldn't quit until I pulled off the distributor wire on the coil, immediately zapping me with its high voltage. After two back-to-back incidents of frying expensive ignition modules and replacing the real culprit (the coil), all seems resolved. Except for the prop.

The prop exchange is an attempt to control the engine speed after the recent engine change. The boost in horsepower has been noteworthy, but so has the RPM. The boat is getting up on-plane fine, but fuel efficiency and engine life is being adversely affected. We hope this prop will solve the problem. There's a science to props involving pitch angles and blade size, but its still mostly "try it, and see what happens."

There's still enough time for a quick test run before it gets dark, so I pull the dock lines while John warms up the engine. I give Bro an ass-boost over the rail onto the aft deck: "We're all aboard!" I yell up to John on the command bridge: "Make 'er go!"

As John steers us out of the docking slip, I climb up to the command bridge to join him. Bro will stay down on the aft deck, head draped over the rail in his normal boating pant.

"Someday we'll be able to tell younger people how we used to go out on nights like this just to cruise around," I say. "Just burning gas."

"Getting pretty expensive for that," he replies. "Not many people will be able to afford this much longer, including me. Things are gonna' be a lot different."

"We'll be telling people about how we used to go out on quads and boats just for fun, and they'll say 'No way!'"

The gas crisis is changing the world. Both taxicab drivers in John's family, Rob and Rick, are in the process of buying new Prius hybrids to get their operating costs back under control. John has just sold one of his float cabins, and the price of gas was an unexpected factor in the sale. The cabin site is one of the closest to the Shinglemill Marina, a fuel-conscious location.

Nowhere is the effect of gas prices more evident than pleasure boating. But for now, we cruise around on a gorgeous July evening, circling past the cement breakwater Hulks at the mill pond, under the pretext of checking out the new prop. It passes its test in flying colours, bringing the cruise RPM down to 3500 and preventing overspeed at full throttle.

I get little sleep that night, thinking about Mark Vonnegut, gas prices, ghosts in the old Hulks in the mill pond at the paper mill, and Von Donop.

* * * * *

The next morning, at the hotel restaurant, I see Dave. He's a good friend, but I'm glad that he's busy with a business deal and only waves to me with a "Hi, Wayne." I'm not sure my mouth is capable of any coherent communication after so little sleep. I'll wake up slowly and be safe on the chuck today, but I need to be careful.

I make my way through my morning chores – Canadian Tire, groceries, a last-minute visit to John's house to file my informal float plan. Then it's back to the condo for city-folk tasks – email, and a few business phone calls. I pack up some ice and pop, and I'm on my way.

I walk down to the marina from the condo, carrying minimal supplies for a single night on the chuck. There'll be opportunities to resupply my food at gas stops along the way, in case I decide to stay more than one night.

It takes a few minutes to clean up the boat's cabin from our prop swap the night before – storing tools and putting away the old prop as a spare. I *tap-tap* the face of the old aneroid barometer (no movement, pressure high). Then I bow to my superstitions about a cruise on the sea by giving a squeeze to Mr. Seagull, a plastic toy bird that hangs from ceiling on a two-foot chunk of fishing line. He emits a high-pitched *Squawk*.

Batteries *Both On*, engine start and warming up nicely, lines removed and secured, and I'm on my way. I motor out of the marina a few minutes before one o'clock, and into a nearly unrippled chuck.

On the command bridge, before powering up, I take off my wristwatch and put it in my pocket, where I hope it won't be checked until I need to verify tidal factors. A good coating of sunscreen on my face, arms, and bare legs, and I'm ready to throttle up. My silly looking safari cap drapes my sun-sensitive ears and neck, and a half-full (hopefully, unspillable) plastic cup of ice-choked water sits in the cup holder. It's the perfect day for a cruise north!

The replacement prop gets me on-plane quickly, and I settle in at a quieter cruise than I've been used to lately, 3500 RPM. The GPS shows a comfortable 21 knots.

Approaching Lund, I decide to use my ahead-of-schedule situation to try my luck fishing at the Iron Mines. This is a spot recommended to me by Jim on my first visit to his marine shop. Obviously a newbie at fishing on the ocean, I asked his advise for catching a salmon from my only ocean boat at the time, a sea kayak.

"Well, try this," he said, grabbing a heavy green and silver lure from the shelf. "Just drop it down to the bottom, and jig it up and down. Fish think it's lame, and you might catch a salmon."

"Okay, but I don't even know where to go," I replied.

Jim is always full of free advice, but he probably doesn't encounter many prospective fisherman as new at it as I am.

"Try the Iron Mines. You can launch your kayak at Lund, and paddle down along the cliffs to the south. Can't miss it – a bunch of rusty looking rock and a big cave in the cliff."

Since that day, seven years ago, I've fished the Iron Mines often. Never have I caught anything of significance. Certainly never a salmon. But it sure looks perfect, so I refuse to give up.

I bob in the nearly calm waters up against the cliffs at the Iron Mines, engine running at idle so I can move away as the gentle swells push me closer to shore. I catch a single small rockfish, one of the smallest I've ever seen.

After a few more minutes of fish inactivity, I continue on to Lund, where only one boat is tied at the gas dock. But it's a big one, named *Otter One*. When I arrive, the skipper is scrubbing the side of his boat and cleaning off the rubber fenders that protrude along the side. He offers me a hand with my lines.

"Where are you from?" asks the skipper.

"Powell River," I answer. "You?"

"Vancouver. Headed north."

"Me, too, but probably not as far as you," I say. "That's a great lookin' boat. What make is it?"

"Grand Banks, 42-foot."

"Well, that explains it."

This is a large classic-looking trawler, and this guy looks relieved to be out of the big city. I'm relieved to be out of Powell River.

"Great day for this," says the skipper.

"Well, at least there aren't any crowds," I reply, waving my arm around the rest of the dock.

"Amazing, isn't it?" he replies.

Yes, it's amazing. A bit scary too.

The fuel attendant comes down when I ring the bell. She's young and athletic looking, but somehow grumpy. At least that's my first impression.

When I'm finished filling my tank, I hand the attendant the nozzle and she replaces it in the pump holder. I pay my bill, making small talk she doesn't seem to enjoy.

I'd like to walk up to Debra's art shop to say hello and check on the current stock of my books in her store. But if the fuel attendant is as disgruntled as she seems, going to Debra's will be tough to explain, so I don't. I simply act like I know what I'm doing and start up the ramp.

"Do you mind if I make a quick stop at the general store for a pop?" I ask the fuel attendant over my shoulder.

The store is only a hundred metres from the top of the ramp-to-shore, and there's no one here except my Bayliner and the Grand Banks. No one is inbound to the harbour, as far as I can see. And going to Debra's store is only a minor white lie – it won't take long.

"Would you mind moving your boat over to that dock first?" she asks, pointing to the adjacent finger.

To get to the dock, I'll need to untie my lines, restart the Bayliner, pull all the way around this dock to the other one, and tie up again. Not a big deal, but not a small one either. On a slow day like today, it seems a lot of effort for a quick run to shore.

"No, that's okay," I say, giving in with a disgusted whimper.

"You can just move it over and then go up," she says, none too pleasantly.

"That's okay," I repeat.

How could someone so young and athletic looking be so bitchy. Or is it me?

I spend a few moments in the boat's cabin, putting away the gas sales slip and computing my litres-per-hour. I mark the new hourmeter time on my fuel log, and prepare to depart. A voice from outside is the fuel attendant.

"Can I help you with your lines?" she asks.

It's not a pleasant offer. It's a reminder to get going.

"No, I'll be out in just a minute," I reply.

I linger in the cabin, moving stuff from one side of the boat to other. Nothing really – just making a point.

When I come outside, the Grand Banks is powered up and ready to go. Another small bowrider has pulled in and tied up. Dad is grabbing the green water house to shower down his young son's dirty feet. The young lad stands resolutely, waiting for the cold water on his toes and flip-flops.

"Sorry, sir," says the attendant. "That hose is for servicing boat water tanks only."

Dad looks at her like she's from outer space. But he winds the hose back onto the rack without a word. The Grand Banks wash-down was from the same faucet. Must be the wrong kind of water.

It's an obvious power play that has little logical importance. The young boy holds his position, waiting for the splash that never comes. I can see it in Dad's face, but he doesn't say a thing: "*Who died and left you in charge?*"

I laugh to myself. At least it's not me. In fact, leaving without visiting Debra is no big deal. The weather is great. I'm now far out of town and about to leave this small remnant of humanity. All is well in my world, and the rest of the world is someone else's problem. I try to forget about Mark Vonnegut.

* * * * *

As I clear Lund Harbour, I continue in idle while I make a final telephone call. Margy answers on her cell phone as she motors along the busy highway through North Vancouver, quickly telling me to hold on a minute while she pulls off at the next exit. I try to imagine her in the midst of four-lane traffic, trying to dodge other vehicles. Society is expanding at a tremendous pace, and I'm not sure I'm capable of adopting to it.

When Margy returns to the phone, she explains that she has just exited the Langdale ferry on her way to Bellingham. As we're finishing up our conversation, the signal starts to break up. It may be on her end, but I also recognize I'm leaving cell territory and the last concentration of people I'll see for a while. It's a good feeling, so I'm not upset when the signal drops completely with an accompanying beep-beep.

I look up Thulin Passage and see no boats, so I elect to take that route. The outside passage of the Copeland Islands would probably be quicker, but I want to see how many boats are anchored in the Copelands, a busy spot during July.

Only one boat is anchored in the marine park, a reminder that gas and the strong Canadian dollar are scaring away the Americans. Even the recreational trawlers from nearby Vancouver are being affected by the price of fuel.

Abeam Sarah Point, I head directly towards Squirrel Cove. If there's space at the small government dock, I'll stop at the cafe for lunch-dinner, preserving my reserve of food for a possible extension of this voyage.

The water has gotten lumpy since leaving the Iron Mines, but Desolation Sound and the surrounding plethora of islands usually keeps the lumps down, and today is no exception. I cruise towards Squirrel Cove in fairly tranquil seas.

It's near low tide when I arrive at the government dock, and it's pretty full. This is a small docking facility, so the fact there are even a few spaces reinforces my perceptions of a slow marine economy. All but one of the open spots are on the inside of the main finger, and it looks pretty shallow. The one outside spot seems big enough for the Bayliner, but it's tucked up close to the towering wooden pilings, which looks tight. I shift into neutral and float near the dock, waiting to see if anyone is about to leave. There are several boats with lots of activity, but I can't tell whether they're arriving or departing.

While I drift and wait, a red and white water taxi, a few feet bigger than my Bayliner, arrives and heads directly for the open outside spot. He moves in quickly and precisely. Once he's docked, I notice plenty of clear space off his bow and stern. I would've fit in there easily.

Although the water taxi keeps his engine running, indicating he'll be leaving soon, I decide to sample the water behind the dock. There's more deep water here than I expected, so I try turning around to put my port side to the dock. It's the easiest side for me to dock, and the torque side-forces of my prop favor maneuvering to this side, but

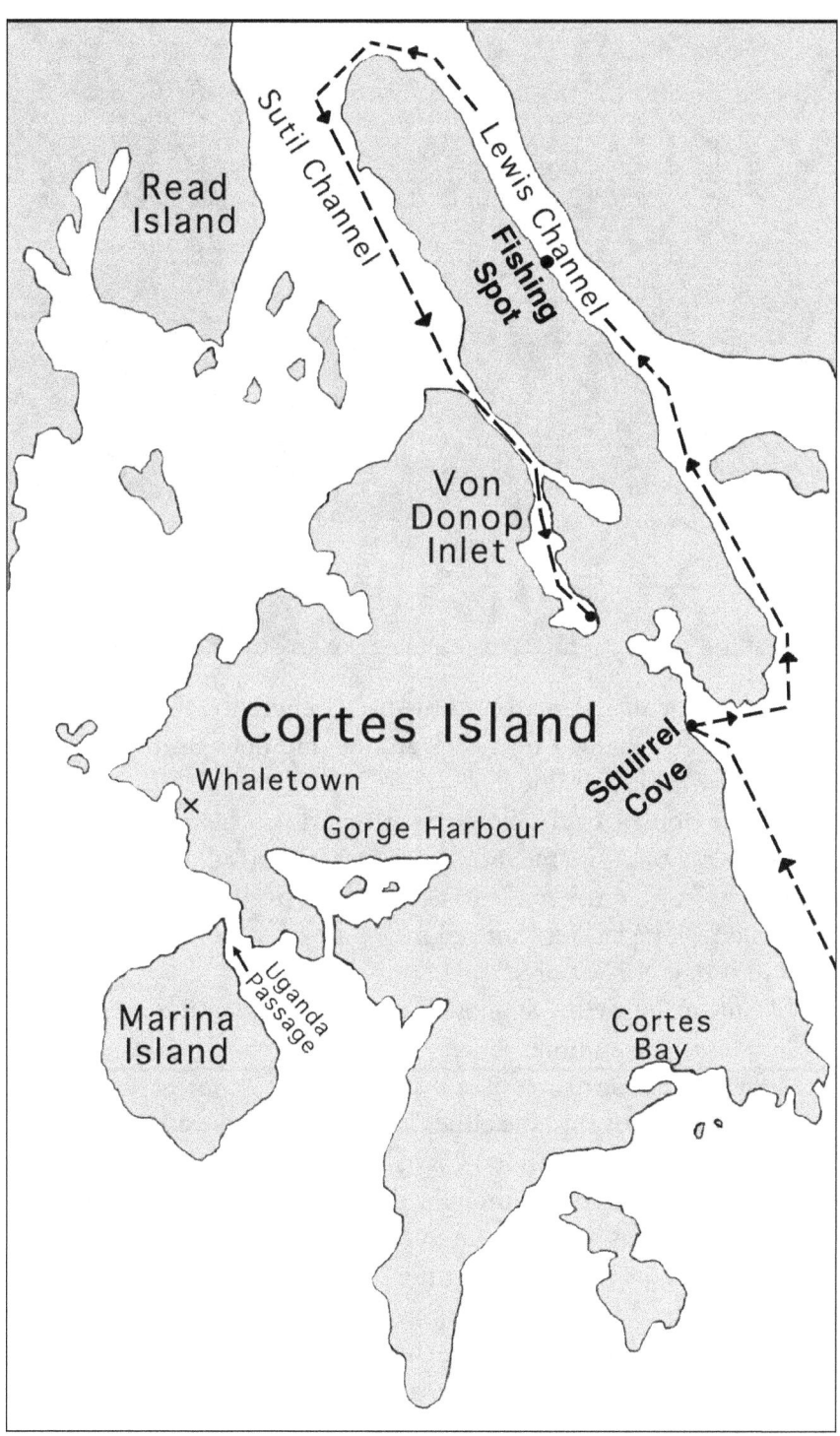

I fumble a bit in the narrow turn-space between the dock and the shallow water. Finally, I turn back around and dock on the starboard side, which works out fine.

A bare-headed bald fellow is washing down his sailboat on the outside berth opposite me, but he ignores my arrival, probably out of courtesy to my clumsy maneuvering. Once I begin to tie up my lines, he speaks as if he has just noticed me.

"Great day, eh?" he says.

"Beautiful," I agree. "Supposed to hold the rest of the week."

"We'll see. No summer so far."

"Last year I wasn't sure there would ever be a summer," I reply.

"Not sure about this one either," he says. "Makes you wonder."

It does make you wonder. Global warming, weird weather, and a gas crisis. Mark Vonnegut thought the end of the world was at hand in surer times than this. But I'm in the sun, with my boat, and on the chuck. No problems. Or at least the problems seem to be dissipating by the minute.

The deck of the Cove Restaurant is barren of patrons, except for me and three locals kicked back over their beers. The sun is warm on my back, and the view of the snow-capped mountains of Desolation

Sound is spectacular. Even the menu prices are reasonable. Maybe that's the way it is during a season when there are few tourists.

On the way back to my boat, walking down the ramp to the government dock, I notice the female wharfinger checking boat names and locations. This woman is older than the young fuel attendant at Lund, and I hope she's friendlier.

"Just in time," I say. "Do I owe you anything for a one-hour stay?"

"Leaving now?" she asks. "We could just call it a half-day fee."

She says it with a lilt in her voice that tells me she isn't serious. Nor is she grumpy. This is the way it should be.

"Oops, I meant to say it was fifty-nine minutes," I reply.

She laughs and continues on her rounds. I untie my boat and am on my way.

* * * * *

Starting up Lewis Channel on the east side of Cortes Island marks a sense of change. This passage feels more isolated, more northerly, and a noticeable difference from the more traveled waters of Desolation Sound to the south. Even the water feels different, more tidal-prone and filled with salmon, at least according to the supposed experts.

Halfway to the turn at the northeast tip of Cortes, I pass abeam two small boats on my left. These are fisherman, working the water along the shore. One is trolling along the cliff, and the other is casting towards the shore. Both boats are confined to a small section of the channel, and I notice the shallow-water shading on my GPS map. This is likely salmon country, so I note its location for my trip back south through here tomorrow.

Rounding the northeast tip of Cortes Island, it's a straight shot to the entrance of Von Donop Inlet, hidden from view without a chart. I slow to no-wake speed in the narrow passage and proceed inward along the lengthy winding channel.

Nearly all the way into the inlet, I see my first anchored boat, then another, along the west shore. I'm looking for anchorage at the head of the inlet, the south end, and I'm not disappointed. This area can be busy in the summer, but today there's plenty of space to swing in a variety of locations. Although ten boats are anchored here, four of them rafted together, there's a perfect spot near the east shore that will remain in sunlight right up to sunset. I drop anchor in 20 feet of water.

My anchor doesn't hold, so I maneuver around, looking for better bottom without sacrificing this position. Again, the anchor drags when I back up. But there's no wind, and the marine forecast is for only a light breeze in the nighttime hours. So I accept what is pretty much a day hook on a short rode, using the weight of the anchor as holding power. It wouldn't work in unprotected water, but it should be fine here.

As soon as I'm finished with my multiple anchor attempts, I break into the ice chest and pour myself a Coke. On a hot day, it's a welcome tradition to grant myself an ice-filled glass of cola upon arrival in a new anchorage. It tastes great!

Then I settle into a lawn chair on the aft deck, reading the *Globe and Mail* newspaper I picked up at Squirrel Cove at the inflated price of $2.25. It's worth it.

After finishing the newspaper, I read some more from Mark Vonnegut's book about Fiddlehead Farm and his experiences in Powell River. The latter part of the book is mostly about his bouts with schizophrenia. It's enough to keep my attention, but I find myself dozing as I read, a victim of too little sleep last night. Unlike Mark,

I'm able to return to a normal sleep cycle. I'm in the V-berth just as the sun drops below the horizon. The fresh marine air drifts through the overhead hatch, which is covered by a mosquito net. I'm out like a light in just a few seconds.

* * * * *

I wake up at 1 am, and drag myself out of the V-berth to check the night sky. It really is a dragging process, since I haven't enough headroom to sit upright in this bed, so I have to pull myself aft, scooting on my backside until I can latch my legs over the edge of the berth. I step out onto the aft deck, where I'm facing south, and there are lights everywhere. Most of them are in a horizontal line, and I recognize them as anchor lights, but an equally bright beam is out of sequence – thirty degrees above the waterline. It's Jupiter, shining as bright as the rest of the anchor lights.

Above me, the Summer Triangle is rotating across the sky. Vega is already well past the zenith. The Milky Way extends from Cassiopeia in the northeast to Scorpius in the south, splitting just below the Northern Cross (Cygnus). A beautiful night under the stars.

* * * * *

I get back to sleep easily, and don't awaken again until sunlight begins streaming through the overhead hatch at 7 o'clock. I stretch, and then climb out of the V-berth. I check the barometer. Tap-tap: high and rock solid. But when I turn on the VHF radio, the marine forecast bodes a change – clear skies will continue, but fair-weather northwesterly winds are scheduled to build to gale force later in the day. That's enough reason to sacrifice a quiet morning in this anchorage and get started back to Powell River. Besides, if I time it right, I should be able to fish the salmon spot I noted in Lewis Channel near the cliffs. I raise anchor and am gone by nine-thirty.

Starting south through Lewis Channel, the wind is starting to pick up, diverted down the passage by the rising northwesterlies. I pass a small fishing boat along the western cliffs, just above the spot I saw the fishing activity yesterday. As soon as I pass, I shift into idle and then neutral, and begin rigging up my poles.

One pole is already set for trolling, with a Deep-6 (a v-shaped wedge to drag my hook deep), flasher, and cop-car lure. It's well short of downrigger efficiency, but it should serve to get me near the salmon, if they're here. While drifting with the wind, still well offshore, I toss my line into the water and let the reel unwind under the weight of the setup. I install a plastic trolling rod holder, slipping it into the slot in the deck's rail. I wait for the *click* of the rod holder as it engages its mount, but there's none. So I wiggle the plastic holder a bit, and feel it slide into the slot. Then I place the fishing rod in the cylindrical holder, facing forward to assure a firm grip.

Now I climb up to the command bridge, and cast out with my other pole. This line will be used for drift-casting against the rocky shore, and I should be able to manipulate it as I drive. But I'll have my hands full, solo in this boat with two rods in action, one of which is down on the aft deck.

I shift back into gear and start closer to the cliffs. I fight the boat a little, trying to jostle into position and keep the bow down the channel. Since the waves are getting more intense now, I'm being pushed pretty fast, so I occasionally shift into neutral and just drift. The drift itself is an ideal trolling speed, but it's impossible to keep the boat straight without a little power on the prop. So I'm in and out of gear, turning here and there, while working my drift-casting line. At that moment, I suddenly realize I have two lines in the water with only one person aboard, and that may not be legal. Or is it?

I'm used to being in this exact same situation with Margy aboard. Not only can she assist with maneuvering and watching for obstacles, it also makes two fishing poles for two people obviously legal. Now I'm not so sure of my situation. But there are no other boats in sight, and I doubt Fisheries is concerned with me. Still maybe I should pull in my drift-casting line.

Before I can make a decision, God decides for me. Down on the aft deck, the trolling reel starts to sing!

The high-pitched whirl of the reel indicates one of two things: either I've hooked a salmon or snagged a rock. Based on my past experience, it's surely a snag. When I look down at the aft deck, the line is zipping off the reel quickly, and there's only so much line before it reaches the end.

I return to the first priority of driving the boat, since I'm now slipping dangerously close to shore. *Snap!* – I hear the crack of what might be my pole, and immediately look down at the aft deck, just in time to see the yellow-and-black pole go airborne and rearward over the transom. The *Snap!* was the sound of the plastic rod holder slipping loose and tilting rearward, allowing the fishing pole to immediately leave the scene. It hits the water and seems to float for a few seconds, semi-buoyant for the moment, but eventually headed down.

I immediately shift into neutral, but I'm drifting fast with the wind, and the pole is sinking behind me. Maybe there's still a chance to retrieve it? I shift into reverse, and give the engine a short burst of power, trying to back up or at least stop my forward plunge. *Zing!* – this time it's the other reel, my drift-casting pole that's still held in my left hand. Have I caught a snag with this one too? Worse! – the line is in the prop (which is now rotating in reverse), and it's rapidly winding itself into a disaster!

I fumble with the controls, getting the power back to idle and finally into neutral. But at least 50 metres of very heavy line (60-pound-test) has wrapped around the prop. And now that I'm in neutral, I'm headed for the cliffs!

There's a relatively clear spot right around the next point, and it looks calm in the eddy behind the promontory. So I aim for it, giving a short burst of power to guarantee hitting my mark. *Zing!* – more fishing line in the prop. Now a brief spurt of reverse to stop the boat. *Zing!* – more line spools off the reel.

But I'm stopped, drifting in the quiet water of this protected small bay. One pole is gone and not worth hunting. Thick fishing line is wrapped every-which-way around my prop. I always fish the ocean with the heaviest of line, just in case I catch a whale.

I think about pulling the prop off the stern drive. And I could do it, thanks to my recent training by John. But this quiet recess in the waves won't remain settled when the next boat passes by. And while I pull the prop, I'll be completely without power for an extended period of time. It's probably best to see if I can unwind and cut as much of the line as possible and drag the rest home with me. I've watched John do this before with his Yamaha outboard, when Margy wrapped a lot of fishing line around his prop: "I sure caught a big one," said Margy, as John worked for ten minutes rotating the prop and unwinding the line.

I raise the stern leg, using the electric tilt, and then launch *Mr. Bathtub* so I can get at the prop. The dinghy bobs on a rope nearby, bumping against the rocks. Kneeled on the swim-grid, I can get at the prop, and I immediately find a birds-nest of thick plastic line. It's wrapped around the blades and the shaft in a hodgepodge of directions caused by my forward-reverse shifting of the engine. With the engine now in neutral, I'm able to rotate the prop and uncurl a lot of line, but much of it still remains, too tight on the shaft to unwind. I attack the mess with a knife, cutting where I can't unwind. There's undoubtedly a lot of line still encased between the prop and it's shaft.

Here comes a boat! What will be worse? – someone seeing me in this embarrassing situation or the wake the boat as it passes? Answer – the wake! The Bayliner and *Mr. Bathtub* rub against each other, and the dinghy goes crunch-crunch against the rocks, but we ride it out without significant damage.

Things settle down. I've done as much as I can without removing the prop, which I'm not about to attempt here. I lower the leg and pull the dinghy back aboard and strap it into position. Engine start is normal, and so is the shift into forward. I move slowly out of the protected bay, out into the rougher waters. Then I power up, watching the gauges. All is normal.

Soon I'm on-plane and headed south. I haven't yet needed to remove a prop at sea. But I could, if I had to. And when I get home, I'll get a personal test of the technique, safely in the harbour at Westview Marina.

As for my attitude – it's a lot better. It's amazing what a few hours on the water can do to get me out of a city-induced funk. The lost fishing pole and the near-disaster with the line wrapped around the prop (to say nothing about being crunched against the rocks) seem almost inconsequential. Which makes me feel bad about Mark. He came so close to being able to enjoy the immense beauty of this region, but never quite got there. The pressures of society are tough for me to handle, but I'm on the water where I belong – healthy, happy, and not quite schizophrenic.

Epilogue

Getting Out There

One of the biggest lessons I've learned about boating in recent years is the importance of accessibility. At first, I was immune to the problems caused by the lack of immediate access to the water. I possessed two boats, one moored in a fresh water marina (Powell Lake) and the other in the salt chuck (Westview). It was a simple matter to hop aboard either boat and navigate on out for a boating adventure, no matter how short notice it might be.

Others have a different idea of accessibility, and it works fine for them. Many of my friends park their boat on a trailer in their back yard, ready to go at a moment's notice. Of course, this requires a degree of confidence in pulling a trailer and launching from a ramp. For me, such confidence is still lacking. Besides, it's tough to store your rig in the back yard when you don't have one.

These days, *Halcyon Days*, my 24-foot Bayliner, moves from salt water to fresh with the seasons, allowing it to serve as an alternate all-weather (almost) boat at my float cabin during the winter. When a storm (other than those true behemoths) moves through, I use the Bayliner as a temporary replacement for my smaller Campion for trips to town. This works effectively because boat moorage is free at my cabin.

When docked at the cabin, I can perform routine maintenance right outside my door, and having *Halcyon Days* nearby allows me to monitor the boat to keep it dry during the winter. (A "dry" boat in the winter? – trust me, it takes constant attention to keep the interior dry during the wet season.)

Do it your own way, but make sure it's quick and easy to get to the water. For many, a trailered boat is the ideal solution, but be sure to keep it simple enough that you can get out there whenever you're ready. When you have a chance to depart on a boating adventure, however brief, you want it to be a user-friendly process.

Come up with a plan that will allow you to get out on the water quickly, and take advantage of the brilliance of the sunshine and the glory of coastal BC. Head north, up the strait, and let me know what you find!

Wayne J. Lutz
Email: wlutz@mtsac.edu

◊ ◊ ◊ ◊ ◊ ◊ ◊

Geographic Index

April Point   p.43
Atrevida Marker   57, 81, 155
Atwood Bay   p.119, 121, 123
Baker Passage (Hernando Island)   p.184, 194
Beazley Passage   p.34-35, 123
Big Bay (Stuart Island)   p.123
Bliss Landing   p.56
Broughton Archipeligo   p.9
Bute Inlet   p.27, 31
Calm Channel   p.31
Campbell River   p.41-42, 45, 58, 61-62, 64, 68
Comox   p.58, 64, 99, 102-103, 159
Coode Peninsula (Okeover Inlet)   p.51
Copeland Islands   p.14, 56, 81-82, 114, 118, 184, 204
Cortes Bay   p.102, 111, 191, 194
Cortes Island   p.30, 32, 83, 124, 133, 181, 184, 191, 194, 196, 207-208
Desolation Sound   p.9, 27, 31, 51, 61. 119, 122-123, 178, 204, 206-207
Dinner Rock   p.14
Discovery Passage   p.41
Dodd Narrows   p.38, 41
Duncan, BC   p.159
East Redondo Island   p.120, 122
Forbes Bay   119-120
Gibsons, BC   p.14, 58, 61, 63-64, 73, 75, 77, 81, 94, 179, 191, 195
Gorge Harbour   p.179, 181-182, 185, 192
Grace Harbour   p.49, 51, 75, 81, 83, 85, 87, 94, 109
Granite Bay (Kanish Bay)   p.39
Harwood Island   p.14, 57, 63
Heriot Bay   p.32, 123-124, 128
Hernando Island   p.66, 133, 136, 143, 184

Geographic Index

Hole in the Wall (Powell Lake)   p.24, 38, 178, 197
Hole in the Wall (Sonora Island)   p.31, 36-37, 115
Homfray Channel   p.119-120, 123
Hoskyn Channel   p.35
Indian Point (Savary Island)   p.143
Iron Mines (Lund)   p.200, 204
Kanish Bay   p.37, 39, 41
Lancelot Inlet   p.11, 16, 47, 87, 91, 93
Lewis Channel   p.30, 207, 210
Lower Rapids (Quadra Island)   p.37-38
Lund   p.14, 56, 117, 155, 184, 200-201, 203
Malaspina Inlet   p.83
Manson's Landing (Cortes Island)   p.191-192
Maurelle Island   p.36
Mink Island (Desolation Sound)   p.119
Mitlenatch Island   p.65, 73, 113, 135-136
Moulds Bay (Quadra Island)   p.128, 130, 135
Mowat Bay (Powell Lake)   p.160, 166, 176, 178
Octopus Islands (Quadra Island)   p.37-39, 115
Okeover Inlet   p.11, 15, 38, 46-47, 49, 51,53, 56, 75, 81, 83, 101, 109, 114
Okisollo Channel   p.39
Porlier Pass   p.41
Quadra Island   p.24, 35-39, 41, 123-124, 130
Read Island   p.32, 35
Rebecca Spit (Drew Bay)   p.133
Refuge Cove   p.27, 81-82, 152-153, 180
Sarah Point (Malaspina Peninsula)   p.27, 118, 145
Savary Island   p.133, 143, 184
Scott Point (Okeover Inlet)   p.49, 51
Seymour Narrows   p.41-42, 44
Shinglemill (Powell Lake)   p.24, 65, 160-162

Geographic Index

Small Inlet (Von Donop Inlet)   p.40-41
Sooke, BC   p.159
Strait of Georgia   p.9-10, 66, 123, 152, 156
Squirrel Cove   p.145, 148, 152, 191, 195-196, 204, 209
Surge Narrows   p.34-36, 123
Sutil Channel (Cortes Island)   p.31, 124
Texada Island   p.79, 133
Theodosia Inlet   p.11-12, 16, 18, 23, 47, 55, 87-88
Thulin Passage (Copeland Islands)   p.14, 81-82, 114, 118, 154, 204
Toba Inlet   p.119, 180
Uganda Passage (Cortes Island)   p.192
Upper Rapids (Quadra Island)   p.37-38
Village Bay (Quadra Island)   p.32, 34
Von Donop Inlet   p.196, 204, 208
West Redondo Island   p.119
Westview Harbour   p.12, 57, 66-67, 77, 111, 112, 116, 132, 144, 156, 183, 197, 199, 215
Willingdon Beach (Powell River)   57
Whale Passage (Cortes Island)   p.32
Whaletown (Cortes Island)   p.32

About the Author

From 1980 to 2005, Wayne Lutz was Chairman of the Aeronautics Department at Mount San Antonio College in Los Angeles. He also served 20 years as a U.S. Air Force C-130 aircraft maintenance officer. His educational background includes a B.S. degree in physics from the University of Buffalo and an M.S. in systems management from the University of Southern California. The author is a flight instructor with 7000 hours of flying experience.

For the past three decades, he has spent summers in Canada, exploring remote regions in his Piper Arrow, camping next to his airplane. The author resides in a floating cabin on Canada's Powell Lake in all seasons, and occasionally in a city-folk condo in Bellingham, Washington. His writing genres include regional Canadian publications and science fiction.

Science Fiction Novels
by
Wayne J. Lutz

Inbound to Earth

Wayne J. Lutz

Echo of a Distant Planet

Wayne J. Lutz

www.PowellRiverBooks.com

Farther Up the Strait is the 8th in a series of volumes focusing on the unique places and memorable people of coastal British Columbia

Order at:
www.PowellRiverBooks.com

Coastal BC Living Blog
PowellRiverBooks.blogspot.com

www.ingramcontent.com/pod-product-compliance
Lightning Source LLC
Chambersburg PA
CBHW071731080526
44588CB00013B/1978